To Our Grandson

Daniel C. Augustine

all our l...

Grandma & G...

25 December /

...ertarian

My Picture Reading Bible
to See and Share

My Picture Reading Bible

to See and Share

V. GILBERT BEERS

A DIVISION OF SCRIPTURE PRESS PUBLICATIONS INC.
USA CANADA ENGLAND

ARTISTS
John Steel
Jack White
Charles McBarron
Cesar E. DeCastro
Darwin Dunham

Revised edition, 1994

Copyright © 1982, 1994 by V. Gilbert Beers

Biblical illustrations, copyright © by Scripture Press
Publications, Inc. 1971-1993

Published by Victor Books/SP Publications, Inc., Wheaton, Illinois.

Library of Congress Catalog Card Number: 82-50562
ISBN: 1-56476-297-1

Printed in the United States of America

To Parents and Teachers

My love for reading began with a love for listening. Long before I learned to read, I learned to listen to my mother read to me. I still vividly remember sitting on her lap as a preschool boy. She read enthusiastically from our only children's book, a colorless Winston Second-Grade Reader.

Before long I had almost memorized every story in that reader. Then my mother began reading poetry, which she loved. Long before I entered school I had been thoroughly exposed to such great poets as Lowell, Longfellow, and Holmes.

But I wish I could also have had a book like this one. We did not have one colorful children's book to stir my interest in God's Word. That memory has encouraged me to work enthusiastically on this book.

There is no good substitute for the read-to-me experience. I know what it did for me. I have also seen what it has done for my own five children. My wife Arlie read daily to each of them for several years. Now each loves books and good literature. But most important, each loves God's Word.

This is a read-to-me book. It is designed for you to read to your child.

Before you begin reading, be sure to spend time with the section "What You Should Know about This Book," beginning on pages 365. It tells you how to get the most from this book.

The title of the book tells you what it is. This is a picture Bible more than a story Bible. It emphasizes picture reading, so that your child may learn to see much that he or she could easily pass over. These stories are shared learning experiences involving you and your child.

More than anything else, this book will help you and your child see and share the Word of God. It will also help your child learn about our Lord Jesus Christ.

Our earnest prayer is that your child will come to a love for God's Word and a love for the Saviour.

Step by Step through This Book

God Makes a Beautiful World *Genesis 1:1-19*   16

God Makes Plants and Animals *Genesis 1:20-31*   18

The Garden of Eden *Genesis 2*   20

Adam and Eve Do Not Obey God *Genesis 3*   22

Noah Builds a Big Boat *Genesis 6*   24

Going on Noah's Boat *Genesis 7:1-16*   26

God Sends a Flood *Genesis 7:17-9:19*   28

The Tower of Babel *Genesis 11:1-9*   30

Abraham Moves *Genesis 11:26-12:9*   32

A Visit to Egypt *Genesis 12:10-20*   34

Abraham Goes Away from Lot *Genesis 13*   36

Angels Visit Abraham *Genesis 18:1-15*   38

A Bride for Isaac *Genesis 24*   40

Isaac Digs Some Wells *Genesis 26:12-33*   42

Jacob Lies to His Father *Genesis 27:1-28:9*   44

Jacob's Dream *Genesis 28:10-22*   46

Joseph's Beautiful Coat *Genesis 37:1-11*   48

Joseph Becomes a Slave *Genesis 37:12-36*   50

Joseph Comes to See the King *Genesis 41:1-45*   52

Joseph Helps His Brothers *Genesis 45:1-15*   54

God Takes Care of Baby Moses *Exodus 2:1-10*   56

Moses Sees a Strange Bush *Exodus 3:1-4:17*   58

Moses Leads God's People *Exodus 5-12*   60

God's People Leave Egypt *Exodus 13:17-18, 21*   62

A Pillar of Cloud and Fire *Exodus 13:21-22*   64

A Trip through the Sea *Exodus 14:1-29*   66

God Gives Special Food *Exodus 16*   68

Water from a Rock *Exodus 17:1-7*   70

The Ten Commandments *Exodus 20:1-21*   72

The Golden Calf *Exodus 32*   74

Gifts for God's House *Exodus 35:1-29*   76

The Promised Land *Numbers 13*   78

Crossing the Jordan River *Joshua 3*   80

God Helps His People *Joshua 6*   82

Joshua Forgets to Pray *Joshua 9*   84

Gideon Sees an Angel *Judges 6*   86

God Helps Gideon *Judges 7*   88

The Story of Ruth *Ruth 1-4*   90

Hannah Prays for a Baby *1 Samuel 1:1-20*   92

Samuel Does God's Work *1 Samuel 1:21-28*   94

God Talks to Samuel *1 Samuel 3:1-18*   96

Samuel Anoints David *1 Samuel 16:1-13*   98

David Fights Goliath *1 Samuel 17*   100

Best Friends *1 Samuel 18:1-4*   102

David Hides from King Saul *1 Samuel 23:19-29*   104

Abigail Brings Food to David *1 Samuel 25:1-35*   106

8

David Is Kind to King Saul *1 Samuel 26*　　108

David Moves the Ark *2 Samuel 6*　　110

David Helps Mephibosheth *2 Samuel 9*　　112

David Forgives a Man *2 Samuel 19:16-23*　　114

David Plans God's House *1 Chronicles 22-26*　　116

Solomon Asks to Be Wise *1 Kings 3:1-15*　　118

Ravens Feed Elijah *1 Kings 16:29-33; 17:1-7*　　120

God Feeds Elijah *1 Kings 17:7-16*　　122

A Boy Comes Back to Life *1 Kings 17-24*　　124

Elijah Prays for Fire *1 Kings 18*　　126

God Whispers to Elijah *1 Kings 19:1-18*　　128

Naboth's Vineyard *1 Kings 21*　　130

A Story of Two Kings *1 Kings 22:1-40*　　132

Elisha Does God's Work *2 Kings 2:1-18*　　134

Pots of Oil *2 Kings 4:1-7*　　136

A Happy Family *2 Kings 4:18-37*　　138

Naaman Obeys *2 Kings 5:1-14*　　140

An Army of Angels *2 Kings 6:8-17*　　142

Helping People Who Hurt Us *2 Kings 6:18-23*　　144

The Boy Who Became King *2 Kings 11*　　146

Giving for God's House *2 Kings 12:1-16*　　148

God Helps Hezekiah *2 Kings 19*　　150

God's Word Is Found *2 Kings 22:1-23:3*　　152

God's Goes with His People *Ezra 7-8*　　154

Nehemiah Prays *Nehemiah 1:1-2:10*　　156

Building a Wall *Nehemiah 2:17-7:3*   158

Ezra Reads God's Word *Nehemiah 8:1-12*   160

This Queen Is Brave *Esther 2-8*   162

Isaiah Obeys God *Isaiah 6*   164

Jeremiah Listens and Obeys *Jeremiah 36*   166

Daniel Says No Thank You *Daniel 1*   168

Daniel's Three Friends *Daniel 3*   170

God Writes to a King *Daniel 5*   172

Daniel in the Lions' Den *Daniel 6*   174

Jonah Runs Away *Jonah 1-3*   176

An Angel Brings Good News *Luke 1:26-38*   178

Mary Visits Elizabeth *Luke 1:39-56*   180

Johns Is Born *Luke 1:57-80*   182

Baby Jesus Is Born *Luke 2:1-7*   184

Angels Appear to Shepherds *Luke 2:8-14*   186

Shepherds Visit Baby Jesus *Luke 2:15-20*   188

Simeon Holds Baby Jesus *Luke 2:21-38*   190

Wise Men Follow a Star *Matthew 2:1-8*   192

Wise Men Give Jesus Gifts *Matthew 2:9-12*   194

Mary and Joseph Go to Egypt *Matthew 2:13-18*   196

Coming Home to Nazareth *Matthew 2:19-23*   198

Jesus Helps Joseph *Luke 2:39-40*   200

The Boy Jesus Obeys *Luke 2:41-52*   202

John Tells about Jesus *Matthew 3:1-12*   204

Jesus Is Baptized *Matthew 3:13-17*   206

Jesus Is Tempted *Matthew 4:1-11*   208

Jesus in God's House *John 2:13-16* 210

Jesus Talks to Nicodemus *John 3* 212

Jesus Heals a Boy *John 4:43-54* 214

Jesus Reads God's Word *Luke 4:16-30* 216

Jesus Helps Peter Fish *Luke 5:1-11* 218

Four Friends Follow Jesus *Matthew 4:18-22* 220

Jesus Heals a Woman *Mark 1:29-34* 222

Jesus Heals Many People *Luke 4:40-44* 224

Jesus Heals a Man *Luke 5:17-26* 226

Jesus Talks to Matthew *Luke 5:27-28* 228

Jesus Eats with Matthew *Luke 5:29-32* 230

Jesus Helps a Man Walk *John 5:1-13* 232

Jesus Heals a Man's Hand *Matthew 12:9-14* 234

Jesus Teaches from a Boat *Mark 3:7-12, 4:1* 236

Men Who Helped Jesus *Mark 3:13-19* 238

Jesus Helps a Soldier *Luke 7:1-10* 240

Jesus Makes a Storm Stop *Mark 4:35-41* 242

This Girl Is Alive Now! *Mark 5:21-24, 35-43* 244

Jesus Feeds Hungry People *Mark 6:30-44* 246

Jesus Walks on Water *Matthew 14:22-33* 248

Jesus Heals Many People *Mark 6:53-56* 250

Jesus Helps a Mother *Matthew 15:21-28* 252

Jesus Heals a Deaf Man *Mark 7:32-37* 254

Jesus Talks with Peter *Matthew 16:13-16* 256

Jesus Looks Different *Matthew 17:1-9* 258

Who Is Most Important? *Matthew 18:1-5* 260

A Man Who Did Not Forgive *Matthew 18:21-35*   **262**

Jesus Heals a Blind Man *John 9*   **264**

A Good Neighbor *Luke 10:25-37*   **266**

Mary and Martha *Luke 10:38-42*   **268**

Jesus Teaches How to Pray *Luke 11:1-4*   **270**

A Lost Sheep *Luke 15:3-6*   **272**

A Boy Who Ran Away *Luke 15:11-24*   **274**

Lazarus Comes Back to Life *John 11:1-45*   **276**

Jesus Helps Ten Lepers *Luke 17:11-19*   **278**

Two Men Pray at God's House *Luke 18:9-14*   **280**

Jesus Loves Children *Mark 10:13-16*   **282**

A Rich Young Man *Mark 10:17-31*   **284**

Jesus' Friends and Helpers *Matthew 20:20-28;*   **286**
Mark 10:35-45

Jesus Helps a Man See *Mark 10:46-52*   **288**

Jesus Forgives Zaccheus *Luke 19:1-10*   **290**

Singing Praise to Jesus *Matthew 21:1-9*   **292**

Jesus Teaches in God's House *Matthew 21:10-27*   **294**

Giving at God's House *Mark 12:41-44*   **296**

Mary Shows Love to Jesus *John 12:1-8*   **298**

Jesus Washes Peter's Feet *John 13:1-17, 34-35*   **300**

Jesus' Last Supper *Luke 22:14-20*   **302**

Jesus Prays in a Garden *Luke 22:39-46*   **304**

Peter Says Something Bad *Luke 22:54-62*   **306**

Jesus Goes before Pilate *Matthew 27:11-26*   **308**

Jesus Dies on the Cross *Matthew 27:38-66*   **310**

Jesus Comes Back to Life   *Matthew 28:1-10*   312

Jesus' Tomb Is Empty   *John 20:1-10*   314

Mary Magdalene Sees Jesus   *John 20:11-18*   316

Jesus Walks with Two Friends   *Luke 24:13-35*   318

Thomas Sees Jesus   *John 20:24-29*   320

Peter Sees Jesus   *John 21:1-17*   322

Jesus Goes Back to Heaven   *Acts 1:9-11*   324

God Heals a Crippled Man   *Acts 3:1-11*   326

Peter Preaches about Jesus   *Acts 5:12-42*   328

Stephen Is a Brave Helper   *Acts 6-7*   330

Philip Teaches a Prince   *Acts 8:26-40*   332

Saul Becomes Jesus' Friend   *Acts 9:1-20*   334

Dorcas Is a Good Helper   *Acts 9:36-43*   336

Cornelius Believes in Jesus   *Acts 10*   338

Peter Gets out of Prison   *Acts 12:1-11*   340

Peter's Friends Pray for Him   *Acts 12:12-17*   342

Paul Helps a Crippled Man   *Acts 14:8-18*   344

Lydia Is a Good Helper   *Acts 16:11-15*   346

A Jailer Believes in Jesus   *Acts 16:16-34*   348

Paul Goes to Athens   *Acts 17:16-34*   350

Priscilla and Aquila   *Acts 18:1-11*   352

People Burn Some Books   *Acts 19:17-20*   354

God Keeps Paul Safe   *Acts 23:12-24*   356

God Takes Care of Paul   *Acts 27*   358

Timothy Is a Good Helper   *Acts 16:1-4; 17:10-15;*   360
1 and 2 Timothy

Onesimus Comes Back Home *Philemon* **362**

What You Should Know about This Book **365**

What is "picture reading"? It's a terrific way to get children involved in learning about God's Word! Discover how to help bring these Bible stories alive for children. Turn to page 365 to find out how.

God Makes a Beautiful World

Genesis 1:1-19

Look at this big beautiful ball in the sky! You live on this ball. It is called the world. If you were standing on the moon, this is how the world would look. You would see the world shine, like the moon does at night. You would also see the stars. The sky is filled with them. Long ago these things were not in the sky. Everything was dark. Then God made the world. He made the sun and moon. He made stars. "Let there be light!" God said. Suddenly there was the world, and sun, and moon. Aren't you glad God made this beautiful world? Aren't you glad He made it for you?

A TIME TO SHARE
1. *What do you like best about our world?*
2. *Are you glad God made our beautiful world?*
3. *Have you thanked Him for doing this?*
4. *Would you like to thank Him now?*

WHAT DO YOU SEE?

This picture of the world shows many places. Can you find the place where you live? If not, ask someone to help you.

WHAT DO YOU SEE?

How many kinds of animals do you see in this picture?
What else do you see? Why do you think these animals
look so happy together?

God Makes Plants and Animals

Genesis 1:20-31

What if there were no animals? The world would be a sad lonely place, wouldn't it? God thought His beautiful world should have lions and tigers. He wanted it to have zebras, giraffes, and elephants. He wanted you to have your favorite dog or cat. "Let the world have every kind of animal!" God said. So there they were, just as God said. He made fish and birds too. He filled the world with trees and plants and green grass. Bright flowers bloomed on the hills. It was so wonderful! What a good place for a sleepy lion to sun himself!

A TIME TO SHARE
1. *Would you like to walk in this place?*
2. *What would you do there?*
3. *Who made all these things?*
4. *Are you happier when you obey or disobey?*

The Garden of Eden

Genesis 2

What is the most beautiful place you have ever seen? God made a place like that. He called it the Garden of Eden. It had trees and flowers. It had animals and birds. "This is your home," God told Adam. He was the first man on the world. God made him from some dust. God also made a woman. Adam called her Eve. God told Adam and Eve to take care of the garden. They had everything they wanted in their beautiful garden. It was like being on vacation all the time.

A TIME TO SHARE

1. Who are the first two people God made?
2. Do you think they were happy? Why?
3. What is the name of their garden home?
4. What would you like to do in this garden?

WHAT DO YOU SEE?

Look at the birds and the plants. Look at the animals.
Which of these do you see around your home? How many
different plants and animals can you find in this picture?

WHAT DO YOU SEE?

Which way are Adam and Eve looking, behind them or
ahead of them? Their beautiful garden home is back
there. Why are they looking back at it? What are they
thinking? What do you see ahead of them?

22

Adam and Eve Do Not Obey God

Genesis 3

How would you like to have everything you need? Adam and Eve did. They should have been happy. They had all the good food they could eat. They had a beautiful garden home. They had everything. God loved Adam and Eve. He wanted them to enjoy the beautiful garden. But one day Satan came to see Eve. He talked about some special fruit. "God says we must not eat it," Eve told Satan. Satan kept on talking about the fruit. Soon Eve wanted it. She knew it was wrong. God had said no. But she ate some. Adam ate some too. Now you see Adam and Eve running from their garden home. God is sending them away. Now they will have to work hard for their food. Don't you think they should have obeyed God?

A TIME TO SHARE
1. *Who are these two people?*
2. *Where are they going? Why?*
3. *What would you like to tell them?*

23

WHAT DO YOU SEE?

How many men do you see in this picture? Which are the neighbors? What do you think they are saying about Noah? Do you see any water near the boat? Where will the water come from?

24

Noah Builds a Big Boat

Genesis 6

Look at those men working! One is Noah. The other three are his sons. The neighbors think Noah and his sons are foolish. Why would anyone build this big boat here? There is no river. There is no lake. There is no ocean. Are Noah and his sons wrong? No, because God told them to build this boat here. God is sending a big flood. Then the neighbors will wish they were on this big boat.

A TIME TO SHARE
1. *Who are the four men at the boat?*
2. *What are these men doing? Why?*
3. *What would you like to say to Noah?*

Going on Noah's Boat

Genesis 7:1-16

Noah and his sons worked on the big boat for many years. One day they nailed the last board on it. The boat was finished. But Noah's work was not finished. "Bring animals and birds into the boat," God said. Noah did what God told him. He brought animals and birds. There was a mother and father of each kind. Think of all the mooing and meowing and barking and chirping! Would you like to have been there when God closed the door of the boat? What would you have said to Noah when the rain began to fall? Noah knew this would happen because God said it would.

A TIME TO SHARE
1. *Why are the animals going on the boat?*
2. *Who helped the animals go there?*
3. *How did Noah know that it would rain?*
4. *Do you do things because God says so?*

WHAT DO YOU SEE?

How many different kinds of animals do you see in this picture? There are two of each kind. Do you know why? Who is the man in the front of the picture? Who are the other three?

God Sends a Flood

Genesis 7:17—9:19

Noah was not surprised when the rain came. God told him it would. The rain pattered on the roof of the big boat. It kept on coming. Soon water covered the ground. Noah's neighbors wished they were on the big boat now. They wished they had listened to God. But it was too late. The rain came down harder. No one had seen so much rain. At last it covered everything in the world. But the animals and birds were safe in the boat. So were Noah and his family. They were glad they had listened to God. How happy they were when the flood was over! When they saw a rainbow they thanked God that He had taken care of them. The rainbow was God's promise. He would never send a big flood like this again.

A TIME TO SHARE
1. *Is the flood over?*
2. *How do you know?*
3. *What are Noah and his family doing?*

WHAT DO YOU SEE?

How many people do you see in this picture? Which one do you think is Noah? What is he doing? Noah's wife is here. So are his three sons and their wives. The flood is over. They are thanking God for keeping them safe.

WHAT DO YOU SEE?

Where do you see bricks in this picture? These bricks are made of mud. They are hard because they are baked in the hot sunlight. But where are the people taking all these bricks?

The Tower of Babel

Genesis 11:1-9

People like to build big things. Look at these people building a tall tower. They are going up higher and higher. They think they will build this tower all the way to heaven. Then they will not need God to get there. Of course they can't do that, can they? Nobody can build a tower that high. God did not like this tower. He did not like what the people were doing. "I will make these people speak different languages," God said. Soon the people could not talk to each other. So they could not work together. The people moved away. They did not finish their tall tower. But they did give it a name. It was called the Tower of Babel.

A TIME TO SHARE
1. *What are these people making?*
2. *How high do they want to make it?*
3. *Why did the people stop doing this?*

WHAT DO YOU SEE?

What are some things Abraham had to take with him when he moved? How many can you find in the picture? Abraham had men to help him. They were servants. How many do you see?

Abraham Moves

Genesis 11:26—12:9

It is moving day! Do you know this man who is moving? It is Abraham. He was also called Abram. God told him to go to a new land. It isn't easy to move. Abraham had so many camels and donkeys and sheep to take with him. But God told him to do it. Nobody says no to a good friend. Abraham and God were good friends. Abraham said he would move, and he did!

A TIME TO SHARE
1. *What did God want Abraham to do?*
2. *Why did Abraham do this?*
3. *Can you think of things God wants you to do?*
4. *What will you do about them?*

WHAT DO YOU SEE?

Which person do you think is Abraham? Which is Sarah?
Who else do you see in the picture? If you moved today
how would you do it? What do you see in this picture that
is different from the way you would move?

34

A Visit to Egypt

Genesis 12:10-20

It is time to move again. Abraham and his wife Sarah are hungry. They cannot find enough food in Canaan. So look what they are doing. They are moving to Egypt. Abraham rides on a camel. Sarah rides on a camel. The servants drive the sheep and cattle. But Abraham is worried. "You are beautiful," he tells Sarah. "The men in Egypt may kill me. They may want to take you away." Abraham wants Sarah to tell a lie. "I am his sister," Sarah told the men in Egypt. But the king of Egypt was angry when he learned the truth. "Get out of here!" he told Abraham and Sarah. When the king says to get out, it is time to go!

A TIME TO SHARE
1. *Where are these people going?*
2. *Why are they leaving their home?*
3. *What will happen to them in Egypt?*

Abraham Goes Away from Lot

Genesis 13

Something is wrong here! These two men are talking about it. Abraham has servants who take care of his animals. Lot has servants who take care of his animals. But Lot's servants want the same green grass that Abraham's servants want. They can't both have it, can they? Lot and his uncle Abraham are talking. "Take what you want first," Abraham told Lot. That was a wonderful thing for Abraham to say. Lot should let his uncle have the best. But he doesn't. He takes the best for himself. What do you think of that?

A TIME TO SHARE
1. *Who is the man with the white beard?*
2. *What is he saying?*
3. *What would you like to tell Lot?*
4. *Should we share the best or keep it?*

WHAT DO YOU SEE?

Look at all the green grass. Why did the servants want it?
Would they argue if the fields were dry and brown? Why
not?

Angels Visit Abraham

Genesis 18:1-15

Do you see these three men with Abraham? They look like men. But they are not. They are angels. "You and Sarah will have a baby," the angels tell Abraham. Do you see Sarah peeking out of her tent? She is laughing. Sarah is 90 years old. Women that old don't have babies, do they? But God is going to give Abraham and Sarah a special baby. They will name him Isaac. He will be a father and grandfather and great-grandfather to some important Bible people.

A TIME TO SHARE
1. *Who are these three people with Abraham?*
2. *What are they telling him?*
3. *Sarah is laughing. Do you know why?*
4. *When God promises something, will He do it?*

WHAT DO YOU SEE?

Sarah and Abraham's home was much different from yours. What they did each day was different too. What do you see in this picture that you do not see at your home?

A Bride for Isaac

Genesis 24

Have you been to a wedding? The bride and her husband looked happy together, didn't they? They met somewhere. They fell in love. Then they decided to get married and told their families. But in Isaac's time, it was not done that way. Someone else looked for the bride. The man in the picture is Abraham's servant. He is choosing a bride for Abraham's son Isaac. The servant talked with God. He asked God to help him find the right girl. So God helped him find this girl, Rebekah. The man will tell the girl and her father about Isaac. He will ask if the girl will marry Isaac. When they say yes he will take Rebekah home to marry Isaac.

A TIME TO SHARE
1. *Who is this man?*
2. *Why has he come to this place?*
3. *What will he ask this girl to do?*

WHAT DO YOU SEE?

Rebekah is working. But what is she doing? Abraham's servant had asked God to show him the right girl for Isaac. The right girl would pour water for his camels. What do you think this servant is going to say now?

Isaac Digs Some Wells

Genesis 26:12-33

These men are working hard, aren't they? They are making a wall. Below it is a deep hole with water in it. The men dug this well with shovels and spades. But some other men are here. Do you see them? They will come to this well. "This is our well!" they will say. They will take it from the men who dug it. Isaac and his men dug the well. They worked very hard. But they will not fight to keep it. Isaac will dig another well instead.

A TIME TO SHARE

1. *What are the men putting around the well?*
2. *Which man do you think is Isaac?*
3. *What will Isaac do when men take the well?*
4. *Would you rather fight or make friends?*

WHAT DO YOU SEE?

How is this well different from wells you have seen?
Which men in the picture dug this well? Which ones will
take it from them?

Jacob Lies to His Father

Genesis 27:1—28:9

Isaac is an old man now. Do you see how white his hair is here? He is blind too. Isaac puts his hand on the head of his son Jacob. He promises something special to Jacob. It is called a birthright. When Isaac dies Jacob will be head of the family. But something is wrong here! Isaac does not know it is Jacob. He thinks this is Jacob's older brother Esau. Isaac thinks he is giving the birthright to Esau. Jacob knows he is lying to his father. Think how angry Esau will be when he does find out!

A TIME TO SHARE
1. *Who are these two men?*
2. *How did Jacob lie to his father?*
3. *Why will Esau be angry about this?*
4. *Why should we not lie to friends or family?*

WHAT DO YOU SEE?

Look at the fur tied to Jacob's neck and arms. His mother tied it there. Esau had thick hair on his neck and arms. Jacob wanted his neck and arms to feel like Esau's. Then his father would think he really was Esau.

WHAT DO YOU SEE?

Look at the things Jacob has with him. What do you think they are? If you saw someone with these things, would you think he was going on a trip? Why?

Jacob's Dream

Genesis 28:10-22

Jacob has run away from home. He lied to his father. He got something special from him. Jacob's brother Esau was angry. He wanted to kill Jacob. That is why Jacob ran away from home. Now Jacob is sleeping. But look! Have you ever seen a stairway like that? It goes up, up, up all the way to heaven. Angels walk up and down on it. God is standing at the top. He talks to Jacob. When Jacob wakes up he knows he is not alone. "This is God's home!" Jacob says. "It is the doorway to heaven." Jacob names this place Bethel. That means "God's house."

A TIME TO SHARE

1. *Who is this man?*
2. *Why did he run away from home?*
3. *What is he dreaming?*
4. *Why do you like to go to God's house?*

Joseph's Beautiful Coat

Genesis 37:1-11

You may not want a coat like this. But Joseph did. His father gave it to him. Look how happy Joseph is as he looks at his coat! Jacob is happy too. Jacob loves Joseph more than any of his other sons. But that brought trouble to the family. The other brothers were older than Joseph. They were angry. They hated Joseph because their father loved him more than he loved them. That isn't the way for a family to live, is it?

A TIME TO SHARE
1. *Where did Joseph get his beautiful coat?*
2. *Why did Jacob give it to him?*
3. *How did this cause trouble?*
4. *Can your family quarrel and be happy?*

WHAT DO YOU SEE?

Two people are happy and two are not. Which do you think are happy? Which two are not? Why are the two brothers not happy?

WHAT DO YOU SEE?

Joseph is walking away from his brothers. Where is he going? Why is he going there? If you were going to Egypt would you travel this way? Why not?

Joseph Becomes a Slave

Genesis 37:12-36

Look at Joseph now! He does not have his beautiful coat. His brothers have it. They will tear it and put blood on it. They will give it to their father. He will think that Joseph is dead. But why would they do that? Because they have sold Joseph. He will be a slave in Egypt. Joseph's brothers hated him. They hated his dreams. They were angry because their father gave more to Joseph than to them. Joseph looks lonely here, doesn't he? But God is going with Joseph. He will take care of him.

A TIME TO SHARE
1. *Where are Joseph's brothers?*
2. *Why do they have Joseph's coat?*
3. *Who is going with Joseph to Egypt?*
4. *Is God with us everywhere we go?*

WHAT DO YOU SEE?

How do you know this man is a king? Some things in the picture tell you. Can you find them?

Joseph Comes to See the King

Genesis 41:1-45

Have you ever had a strange dream? Have you wondered what it meant? Kings have strange dreams too. The king of Egypt had two dreams! He did not know what they meant. He called for his wisest men. But they did not know. Then someone told the king about Joseph. The king sent for him. "I don't know what your dream means," Joseph said. "But God does." Look now! Do you see Joseph? He is telling the king what God said. He is telling him what the dreams mean.

A TIME TO SHARE
1. *Which man is Joseph?*
2. *What is Joseph telling the king?*
3. *How did Joseph know what the dreams meant?*

Joseph Helps His Brothers

Genesis 45:1-15

Joseph's brothers were mean to him. They sold him. They wanted him to be a slave and die. But that was a long time ago. Now they are sorry. Joseph knows they are sorry too. He will take care of them. These brothers and their families are hungry. They have no food. But Joseph has plenty of food. He is rich and famous. So he will share his food with his brothers. Aren't you glad to see a brother like Joseph?

A TIME TO SHARE
1. *Were these brothers mean to Joseph?*
2. *What did they do to him?*
3. *What is Joseph saying to his brothers now?*

WHAT DO YOU SEE?

There are 12 men in the picture. Which one is Joseph? He
is in his house. Do you think he is rich or poor? How can
you tell?

God Takes Care of Baby Moses

Exodus 2:1-10

Look at baby Moses! These happy ladies have found him in the basket. The basket was floating on the river. Do you know why it was there? The king of Egypt wanted to hurt Moses. So Moses' mother hid him in the basket. She asked God to take care of Moses. He did! The lady who is holding Moses is a princess. As you can see, she likes baby Moses. She will take care of him. She will not let the king hurt him. Isn't it wonderful how God took care of baby Moses?

A TIME TO SHARE
1. *Who is holding baby Moses?*
2. *Where did she find him?*
3. *What will the princess do with him?*

WHAT DO YOU SEE?

How many ladies do you see in this picture? Are they happy or sad? Why do you know from this that the king will not hurt baby Moses?

Moses Sees a Strange Bush

Exodus 3:1—4:17

Something strange is happening here! This bush keeps on burning. It never burns up. Moses tiptoes near the bush. He wants to see what is happening. "Moses! Moses!" God calls. He tells Moses to take off his shoes. Moses is afraid. Wouldn't you be afraid if God spoke to you like that? Moses takes off his shoes. He gets down on his knees. He listens. What will God say? "Go to Egypt," God tells Moses. "Lead My people out of there." Moses has been leading sheep. Now he will lead God's people. He will take them to a new home.

A TIME TO SHARE
1. *Who is the man in the picture?*
2. *Why is he on his knees?*
3. *What did God tell Moses to do?*

WHAT DO YOU SEE?

Look on the ground in front of Moses. What do you see?
The long stick is called a staff. Moses used this to take
care of his sheep. But why are Moses' sandals lying on
the ground? Shouldn't they be on his feet?

Moses Leads God's People

Exodus 5–12

How would you like to tell a king what to do?
That's what Moses is doing. God told Moses
what to say to the king. Now Moses is before
the king. "God says, 'Let My people go!'"
Moses tells the king. Moses' people are slaves
in Egypt. They work for the king. But the king
does not pay them. He hurts them. God does
not like that. He wants His people to go away
where the king will not hurt them. So God sent
Moses and Aaron to see the king. God is here,
too, helping Moses and Aaron. Don't you think
Moses and Aaron are glad for that?

A TIME TO SHARE
1. *Who are the two men talking to the king?*
2. *What is Moses telling the king?*
3. *Who is helping Moses and Aaron?*
4. *Would you want God's help if you were Moses?*

WHAT DO YOU SEE?

Why do you think this is a king? Point to some things
that a king has. Moses and Aaron look different from the
king. How do they look different?

WHAT DO YOU SEE?

Do you think you could count these people? How many
do you think there are? Look at all the things they are
taking. What do you see that you can name?

God's People Leave Egypt

Exodus 13:17-18, 21

Look at all these people! They are leaving Egypt. You can't see their faces. But they are happy. They have been slaves for a long time. They worked for the king. He did not pay them. He was mean to them. God did not like this. He sent Moses and his brother Aaron to see the king. God told Moses to say, "Let My people go!" But the king would not let them go. God was angry. He sent trouble 10 times. Then the king said yes. He let the people go away. Now they are not slaves. Moses will lead them on a long trip. God will teach them many good things.

A TIME TO SHARE
1. *Where have these people been living?*
2. *Why are they leaving?*
3. *Who is leading them?*
4. *How would you feel if you were here?*

WHAT DO YOU SEE?

How many of the people are going the same way? What are they following?

A Pillar of Cloud and Fire

Exodus 13:21-22

Do you see something bright in the sky? During the day it looks like a tall cloud. At night it looks like it is on fire. God sent this cloud. He tells it when to move. He tells it when to stop. The cloud goes where God wants it to go. Moses and God's people follow the cloud. God tells them to do this. God shows the cloud where to go. The cloud shows the people where to go.

A TIME TO SHARE
1. *What is this cloud like during the day?*
2. *What is it like at night?*
3. *Who sent the cloud?*
4. *Do you ask God to help you each day?*

A Trip through the Sea

Exodus 14:1-29

Here are people walking through a sea. Have you ever done that? Not many people have. But God is letting His people do it. They are going on a long trip. The king does not want them to go. He and his men are chasing them. But God will not let this king catch them. He tells Moses to hold out his rod. The water of the sea moves apart. Only God can do that, can't He? The people walk on a path through the sea.

A TIME TO SHARE
1. *Where is Moses?*
2. *What is he doing with that rod?*
3. *Who is making the sea move apart like this?*

WHAT DO YOU SEE?

Have you ever seen water pile up like this? Have you ever
seen people walk on a path through the sea? What would
you think if you were here? Would you think that God is
doing this?

God Gives Special Food

Exodus 16

God's people are going on a long trip. They are in a desert now. There are no fields and gardens. There are no stores. So there is no food to eat. "We are hungry!" the people tell Moses. But what can Moses do? He has no food to give them. Moses talks to God. God always listens when we talk to Him, doesn't He? Moses asks God to send food. God listens to Moses. Each morning He sends good food called manna. The people have all they want to eat. That's why these people look happy. Don't you think they should?

A TIME TO SHARE
1. *Who sends this special food?*
2. *What is it called?*
3. *How often does God send it?*
4. *Do you thank God for your food each day?*

WHAT DO YOU SEE?

Do you see little white flakes on the ground? What is it?
Where are the people putting it? Look at the ground.
Why don't gardens and fields grow here?

Water from a Rock

Exodus 17:1-7

"We're thirsty!" God's people told Moses. Have you ever said that? These people are more thirsty than you have ever been. They are walking through a desert. But there is no water. "We will die!" they shout. Poor Moses! He has no water to give the people. He doesn't know where to find water. "Lord, what shall I do?" Moses prays. God tells Moses to hit a rock. Now look what is happening! When Moses hits the rock, water pours out. The people are not thirsty now. That's because Moses did what God told him to do.

A TIME TO SHARE
1. *Did Moses believe God?*
2. *Did he do what God said?*
3. *Do you want to do what God says?*

WHAT DO YOU SEE?

How many plants or trees do you see? Why are there no plants or trees? What kind of land is this? Why do you think the people are so glad to see this water?

The Ten Commandments

Exodus 20:1-21

Here is Moses, standing on a mountain. He is holding two pieces of stone. Do you see the writing on them? God wrote these words Himself. These are 10 rules for us to obey. We call them the Ten Commandments. How would you feel if you were Moses? Wouldn't you want to do everything God says? Wouldn't you want to do what God wrote on these stones? You can! These same rules are in the Bible. God put them there for you and me to obey. Will you?

A TIME TO SHARE
1. *What is Moses holding?*
2. *How many rules are on the stones?*
3. *What should we do about these rules?*

WHAT DO YOU SEE?

Look closely at the words on the stones. You can't read them. They are in a different language. It is called He-brew. Moses and his people spoke this language.

WHAT DO YOU SEE?

Can you find the golden calf? Can you find the stones
with God's rules on them? Which should the people worship, God or the calf? Why?

74

The Golden Calf

Exodus 32

Look at that golden calf! But what are these people doing? These are God's people. They should be praying to God. Now they are praying to a golden calf. Here comes Moses with the 10 rules God gave him. One rule says, "Worship God only." The people are not obeying that! Another rule says, "Don't worship idols." The people are not obeying that either! This golden calf is called an idol. The people are pretending it is like God. Moses is angry. "Obey God!" he tells the people. Some will obey God. Others will not. That's the way it is now, isn't it? But you want to obey God, don't you?

A TIME TO SHARE
1. *What are these people doing wrong?*
2. *Who should they obey?*
3. *Who should you obey?*

Gifts for God's House

Exodus 35:1-29

Do you like to give things to God? These people
do. Look how happy they are. Some are bringing gold or silver. Others are bringing wood or
jewels. Moses and some helpers will build a
beautiful house for God. They will use these
gifts for God's house. It will be a tent. They
will call it the tabernacle. Now you know why
these people are happy. Aren't you happy
when you can give things to God?

A TIME TO SHARE
1. What are the people bringing?
2. What will Moses do with these gifts?
3. Why do the people look happy?

WHAT DO YOU SEE?

What are some of the gifts that you see? How many children do you see? Are they happy or sad?

WHAT DO YOU SEE?

Look at the grapes and fruit. What kind of land was the
Promised Land? How do you know?

The Promised Land

Numbers 13

God promised these people some land. He called it the Promised Land. They could live there. They could build their homes there. But they must first go into the new country. They must fight for it. The people wondered what this land was like. So they sent 12 men to see. Look what these men brought back! "It is a good land," the men are saying. Two of the men say the people should go in. They should take it. But 10 of the men are afraid. They do not believe God will help them. Most of the people listen to the men who are afraid. So the people do not go into the Promised Land. They do not get the beautiful land God wanted to give them.

A TIME TO SHARE
1. *What did God want to give His people?*
2. *Why didn't they accept His gift?*
3. *What good gifts does God want you to have?*
4. *Can you name some good gifts God gives you?*

Crossing the Jordan River

Joshua 3

These people are going across a river. They have no boats. They have no bridge. But they are not getting wet. That's because God made a path through the river. He also helped Joshua. He showed Joshua the way to the Promised Land. Joshua is showing the people the way. Aren't you glad for people like Joshua?

A TIME TO SHARE
1. *What is Joshua doing?*
2. *Do you know people who show you God's way?*
3. *Do you listen to them?*

WHAT DO YOU SEE?

The man in the middle is Joshua. He is showing God's people which way to go. Do you see some priests carrying something? It is covered with a blue cloth that God told His people to make. This is the ark. The priests will wait in the middle of the river until all the people are across.

God Helps His People

Joshua 6

Look at all these people. They are marching around the city of Jericho. Joshua and his people are in the Promised Land now. But they must fight the people of Jericho. They must take the city. God has told them what to do. So they are doing it. Around and around the city they go. The priests carry God's golden chest, the ark. Each day this week they march around the city once. Today they must go around it seven times. Do you see what the priests are doing now? This is the seventh time they have marched around Jericho. They are blowing on their trumpets. The people will shout. In a moment those walls will fall down. The people will go into the city. They will take it. That's because God is helping them.

A TIME TO SHARE
1. *What is the name of this city?*
2. *What will happen to the walls?*
3. *Who will give this city to the people?*
4. *What does God help you do?*

WHAT DO YOU SEE?

How many priests do you see? What are they blowing?
Do you see all the people coming after the priests? What
are the priests carrying?

Joshua Forgets to Pray

Joshua 9

Do you see these people in old clothes? They live in a city called Gibeon. It is in the Promised Land. Joshua and his people have taken some other cities. So these people are afraid. They decided to trick Joshua. They pretended to come from a place far away. "We have heard about your great God. We want to make peace with you," they are telling Joshua. Joshua should ask God about these people. But he doesn't. He says God's people will not fight them. Now Joshua cannot take their city. He will be sorry he did not ask God what to do.

A TIME TO SHARE
1. *What are the people from Gibeon saying?*
2. *Why are they doing this?*
3. *What did Joshua forget to do?*
4. *Will you remember to pray today?*

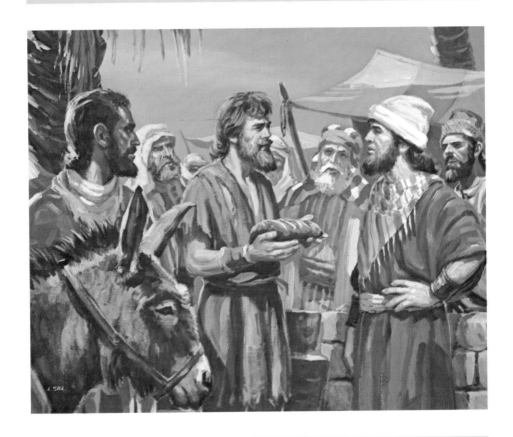

WHAT DO YOU SEE?

A man from Gibeon holds out some bread. It is moldy. He says it was fresh when he left home. He is tricking Joshua. Joshua thinks he is from far away. Which one is Joshua?

Gideon Sees an Angel

Judges 6

Have you ever seen an angel? That's one in the yellow robe. This angel looks like an ordinary person. But he is really an angel. Gideon wants the angel to do something an ordinary person can't do. Gideon says then he will believe that God sent the angel. He gives the angel some food. Do you see what is happening? The angel touches the food. It burns up. Then the angel disappears. Now Gideon knows God sent the angel. He says, "O Lord God, I have seen Your angel." Then God tells Gideon He will help him fight the enemy. Gideon should believe God, shouldn't he? When we know what God wants us to do, we should do it!

A TIME TO SHARE
1. *Which one is the angel?*
2. *What is the angel doing?*
3. *What did God tell Gideon to do?*
4. *Do you try to do what God wants?*

WHAT DO YOU SEE?

What is the angel doing to the food Gideon brought? Can an ordinary person do this? What would you think if you were there?

God Helps Gideon

Judges 7

Gideon has only 300 soldiers. But look down in that valley! There are thousands of other soldiers. How can Gideon hope to win? Do you know? God is helping him. God gave Gideon a good plan. His men are to break clay pitchers. Torches will shine on all the hills. The men blow their trumpets. The soldiers down below see the torches. They hear the trumpets. Now they are afraid. They think Gideon has a bigger army than theirs. They begin to run away. Then they fight each other. Before long, Gideon and his men win. But that is because God helps them.

A TIME TO SHARE
1. *Why are Gideon's men blowing trumpets?*
2. *Why are they carrying torches?*
3. *Who is helping Gideon and his men?*
4. *Who will help you do your work today?*

WHAT DO YOU SEE?

Where are all the torches? Can you find them? What else
do Gideon and his men have?

WHAT DO YOU SEE?

Do you see some wheat still standing in the field? Do you
see some bundles of wheat? There are two men watching
Ruth. One is Boaz. He owns this field. He is a rich man.
He will marry Ruth. He will take care of Ruth and
Naomi.

90

The Story of Ruth

Ruth 1—4

Ruth is picking up stalks of wheat. This is called gleaning. The people who cut the grain missed some stalks. They must leave them on the ground for poor people like Ruth. She will beat the grains of wheat from the stalks. Then she will grind the wheat with stones. It is hard work. But Ruth needs this flour to make bread. Her mother-in-law Naomi is too old to do this. Ruth must find enough wheat to feed Naomi and herself. Don't you think Ruth is a kind, beautiful lady?

A TIME TO SHARE
1. *What is Ruth doing?*
2. *What will she do with this wheat?*
3. *What kind of person is Ruth? Do you like her?*
4. *Do you like to help others as Ruth did?*

WHAT DO YOU SEE?

Hannah is praying in God's house, the tabernacle. How does this look different from your church? The tabernacle was a big tent. It did not have seats where people could sit down. It did not have a pulpit or communion table.

Hannah Prays for a Baby

1 Samuel 1:1-20

Hannah is praying. "Please give me a baby," she asks. Most of Hannah's friends have children. But she does not. Hannah is sad. She wants a baby. She knows God can do this for her. So Hannah came here to the tabernacle. It is God's house. It is a good place to pray. Do you see Eli the priest watching Hannah? He does God's work at the tabernacle. "God will answer your prayer," he tells Hannah. "You will have a baby this next year." Eli is right. God will answer Hannah's prayer. He will give Hannah a baby boy. She will name her baby Samuel.

A TIME TO SHARE
1. *What is Hannah asking God to do?*
2. *Who is watching her?*
3. *What does Eli tell Hannah?*
4. *Do you like to pray in God's house?*

Samuel Does God's Work

1 Samuel 1:21-28

Look at this happy boy. He is Samuel. Do you remember how Hannah prayed for a baby boy? God heard her prayer. He gave her a baby and she named him Samuel. But Samuel is not a baby now. He is old enough to help Eli do God's work. He is staying here at the tabernacle. Do you see what he is doing here? He is cleaning lamps. Do you see Samuel smiling? He is glad he can help Eli do God's work.

A TIME TO SHARE
1. *Who is this boy?*
2. *What is he doing?*
3. *Why isn't he home with his family?*
4. *How can you help at God's house?*

WHAT DO YOU SEE?

There are stacks of lamps near Samuel. Can you find them? Samuel's people did not have electric lights. They did not have wax candles. They put olive oil in these lamps. The lamps were made of clay. They put a string in the olive oil. When the string was lit, it gave light.

God Talks to Samuel

1 Samuel 3:1-18

Samuel should be sleeping. But he isn't. Someone is calling his name. "Samuel!" Samuel
looks. But he does not see anyone. Who is calling him? Samuel runs to Eli. But Eli did not
call him. Samuel goes back to bed. But Someone calls his name again. "Samuel!" Samuel
looks. But he does not see anyone. He runs to
Eli again. But Eli did not call him. This happens one more time. Now Eli knows what is
happening. "God wants to talk to you," Eli
tells Samuel. "When He calls, listen to Him."
God does call again! "Samuel!" Then God tells
Samuel something special. He wants Samuel to
do Eli's work when Samuel is older. Samuel
will do special work for God.

A TIME TO SHARE
1. *Who is this boy?*
2. *What does he hear?*
3. *What is God telling him?*

WHAT DO YOU SEE?

Does Samuel's room look like yours? What is in his room
that is also in your room? How is his room different from
yours?

WHAT DO YOU SEE?

Samuel is pouring olive oil from an animal horn. This horn once grew on a goat or cow. Do you see how fancy it is? Samuel filled it with olive oil. Do you see him pouring this oil on David's head?

Samuel Anoints David

1 Samuel 16:1-13

Do you see the man with the white beard? He is Samuel. Now he is an old man. Samuel is the most important man in the land. He is even more important than King Saul. Samuel talks with God. Then he tells God's people what God wants. Some of the people do what God wants. Some do not. King Saul should do what God wants. But he doesn't. God does not like this. He wants a king who will obey Him. God tells Samuel to go to David's house. He tells Samuel to pour olive oil on David's head. This is called anointing. It shows that David will be the next king.

A TIME TO SHARE
1. *Which one is David?*
2. *What is Samuel doing to him?*
3. *What does this mean?*
4. *How would you feel if you were David?*

David Fights Goliath

1 Samuel 17

Look at that giant! Have you ever seen such a big man? How would you like to fight him? He has a big spear and shield. He has a helmet and sword. How can David fight him with that little sling? The soldiers in David's army are afraid of this giant. His name is Goliath. That sounds big, doesn't it? But David is not afraid. "God will help me," David says. David whirls a stone around and around in his sling. He whips the stone toward Goliath. Goliath falls to the ground. When Goliath's soldiers see that, they run away. God has helped David win.

A TIME TO SHARE
1. *What does Goliath have with him?*
2. *What does David have?*
3. *Who is helping David?*

WHAT DO YOU SEE?

Do you see Goliath's soldiers behind him? Can you count the spears and swords? There are too many, aren't there? How would you like to be David now?

Best Friends

1 Samuel 18:1-4

The young man in the green robe is Prince Jonathan. His father is the king. Jonathan wants David to be his best friend. He thinks David is brave. Do you know why Jonathan thinks that? Do you remember how David fought the giant Goliath? He was braver than any soldier in the army. He won too! "Let's be best friends," Jonathan tells David. Jonathan gives David some special gifts. He gives David his sword, his bow, his robe, and his belt. These special gifts show David that Jonathan really wants to be his best friend. Best friends do nice things for each other, don't they?

A TIME TO SHARE
1. *Which one is David?*
2. *What is Jonathan giving him?*
3. *What does Jonathan want?*
4. *Do you do nice things for your best friend?*

WHAT DO YOU SEE?

Can you see three of Jonathan's gifts? What are they?
What else do you see here?

David Hides from King Saul

1 Samuel 23:19-29

Look at King Saul sitting there. He is jealous. Isn't that strange for a king to be jealous? A king usually has everything he wants, doesn't he? Saul is jealous of a young man called David. He knows David will be king someday. Saul does not want that. He wants to be king as long as he is alive. Then he wants his son Prince Jonathan to be king. King Saul is trying to kill David. David is hiding and God is taking care of him.

A TIME TO SHARE

1. *Why does Saul want to hurt David?*
2. *Who will keep him from doing this?*
3. *Do you thank God for taking care of you?*

WHAT DO YOU SEE?

David is hiding from Saul. This man has come to tell
Saul where to find David. Do you see Saul's spear? Do
you see his soldiers with spears? God will protect David
from all of these.

WHAT DO YOU SEE?

Point to all the food Abigail brought. There are loaves of
bread, bunches of figs, corn, raisins, and meat.

106

Abigail Brings Food to David

1 Samuel 25:1-35

David is hiding from King Saul. The king wants to kill him. Saul wants to kill some other men too. So they are hiding with David. These men hide in caves. They hide in the desert. They often help the people who live near them. One day they stopped some robbers. These men were trying to steal sheep from Nabal. Nabal is very rich. He is also very selfish. He will not share his food with David and his men. Nabal's wife Abigail does not like this. She is sorry Nabal is so selfish. Do you see what she is doing? She is bringing food to David and his men. Don't you think Abigail is a kind lady?

A TIME TO SHARE

1. *Which person is Abigail?*
2. *What is she bringing to David?*
3. *Why is she doing this?*
4. *Who gives you food each day?*

WHAT DO YOU SEE?

Can you find Saul's spear? Can you find his water jug?
David is kind to King Saul, even though Saul wants to
hurt him.

David Is Kind to King Saul

1 Samuel 26

Saul is chasing David. Saul wants to kill David. He is afraid David will be king. Saul wants to be king as long as he lives. Then he wants his son Jonathan to be king. But now it is night. Saul is sleeping. His soldiers are sleeping too. While they sleep David and a friend tiptoe into Saul's camp. "Let me kill King Saul!" David's friend whispers. "No!" David answers. David takes Saul's spear and water jug. He climbs on a tall hill. "Look what I have!" David shouts. Saul looks. His soldiers look. They see the jug and spear. King Saul is ashamed. David could have killed him. But he didn't. So King Saul goes home. He does not chase David for a while.

A TIME TO SHARE
1. *Does Saul want to hurt David or help him?*
2. *Does David want to hurt Saul?*
3. *Does anyone want to hurt you?*
4. *What should you do to that person?*

David Moves the Ark

2 Samuel 6

King David is certainly happy, isn't he? He is singing and dancing and playing a harp. David is king now. But that is not why he is singing and dancing. He is bringing the ark to Jerusalem. It is a golden chest covered with a cloth. God told His people to make this golden chest. King David wants it in Jerusalem with him. He wants to please God. This is one way to do it.

A TIME TO SHARE
1. *What is King David doing?*
2. *What are the people behind him carrying?*
3. *Why is David bringing the ark to Jerusalem?*

WHAT DO YOU SEE?

Do these people look happy or sad? Does David look happy or sad? Why is everyone so happy? Doing things that please God makes us happy, doesn't it?

David Helps Mephibosheth

2 Samuel 9

The young man with the crutch is Mephibosheth. His father was Prince Jonathan, David's best friend. Jonathan was killed when this boy was little. A woman was carrying Mephibosheth. She was afraid. She tried to run, but fell. Mephibosheth fell too. His feet and legs were hurt. He could not walk well after that. Now he is a young man. He is here with King David. "Don't be afraid," David tells him. "I want to help you." Mephibosheth is happy. David will take care of him. He will have good food and clothing. He will live in the king's house.

A TIME TO SHARE
1. *What will David give Mephibosheth each day?*
2. *Should Mephibosheth thank David?*
3. *What do your parents give you each day?*
4. *Do you thank them? Will you do it now?*

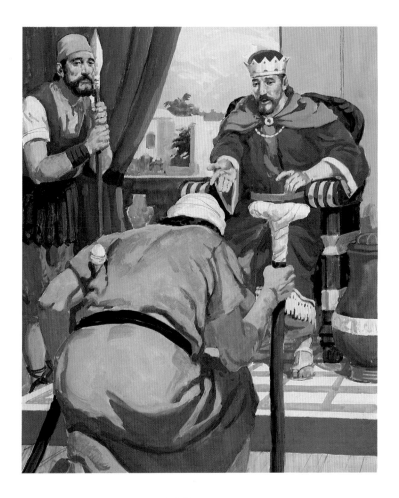

WHAT DO YOU SEE?

What kind of house is this? Do you think King David is
rich or poor? Why do you think this?

David Forgives a Man

2 Samuel 19:16-23

Here comes a man named Shimei. He is afraid. One day he said some terrible things to King David. He called King David some terrible names. David could have killed him. Most kings would have done that. But David didn't. Now Shimei is sorry he said those things. "Forgive me!" Shimei begs. "I forgive you," David says. That's what God says to us, isn't it?

A TIME TO SHARE
1. *Which man is King David?*
2. *What is Shimei asking David?*
3. *What is King David telling him?*
4. *Does someone want you to forgive?*

WHAT DO YOU SEE?

The river behind David is the Jordan River. David has been living on the other side of this river. Some men tried to kill him, so David left his palace to hide. Now it is safe for David to come back home.

David Plans God's House

1 Chronicles 22–26

King David lives in a beautiful palace. It is made of stone and cedar wood. "But God's house is only a tent," David says. He wants God's house to be nicer then his own house. David talked with his friend Nathan. This friend talks to God. But God will not let David build a beautiful house for Him. David's son Solomon must do it. David helps Solomon plan God's house. Do you see David talking to the workers about it here? He is helping Solomon get the wood and stone and things to build it. God's house will be beautiful. That's the way it should be.

A TIME TO SHARE

1. What does David want to do?

2. Who said that he can't do this?

3. What is David doing here?

4. What can you do to make God's house better?

WHAT DO YOU SEE?

How many men in the picture are helping to build a
beautiful house for God? Which man is King David?

WHAT DO YOU SEE?

How many different things do you see in Solomon's room? What is that man doing in the doorway?

Solomon Asks to Be Wise

1 Kings 3:1-15

King Solomon is sleeping. He is dreaming a special dream. God is talking to Solomon in his dream. "I will give you a wonderful gift," God tells Solomon. "What would you like?" Solomon can ask for gold or silver or jewels. He can ask to be famous. He can ask to be a mighty soldier or leader. But these would all be gifts for him. Solomon thinks about this. He is king. He rules over thousands of people. "Help me be a wise king," Solomon answers. This gift will help his people. God is pleased. "You will be wise," God says, "I will make you rich and famous too."

A TIME TO SHARE

1. What did God say He would give Solomon?

2. What did Solomon ask God to give him?

3. Why was God pleased?

4. Do you ask God for things that please Him?

Ravens Feed Elijah

1 Kings 16:29-33; 17:1-7

Elijah is God's friend. Most of Elijah's neighbors are not like he is. They do not want to be God's friends. Even the king does not want to be God's friend. The king thinks a statue called Baal is more powerful than God. He thinks Baal sends the rain and makes the crops grow. What can Elijah do? How can he show King Ahab that only God can do these things? Elijah talks to God. Then Elijah tells the king what will happen. "God will stop the rain," he says. "It will not rain until I say so." Do you see Elijah hiding here by a brook? There is no rain. The crops are not growing. So people do not have food. Look at those ravens. They are bringing Elijah food. God is taking care of Elijah.

A TIME TO SHARE
1. *What is this raven bringing to Elijah?*
2. *Why is it doing this?*
3. *Who is sending food to Elijah this way?*
4. *How does God give your food to you?*

WHAT DO YOU SEE?

Do you see grass and flowers and trees? Why not? What is happening to the weather here?

WHAT DO YOU SEE?

Do you think this woman and her son are rich or poor?
Why? What do you see?

God Feeds Elijah

1 Kings 17:7-16

There has been no rain for a long time. Crops will not grow. People have almost no food to eat. God sent ravens with food for Elijah for a while. Now God cares for Elijah in another way. God has sent Elijah here to see this woman. "May I have some bread and water?" Elijah asks. The woman looks sad, doesn't she?

"I have no bread," she answers. "I have only a little flour and olive oil. I will make some bread with it. Then my son and I will starve." Do you know what Elijah is telling the woman?

"Share your bread with me," he says. "God will not let you starve." The woman shares her bread with Elijah. Then she has a surprise. Each day she has enough flour and oil to make more bread. God feeds Elijah. He feeds the woman and her son.

A TIME TO SHARE
1. *Who is this man?*
2. *What is he telling the woman?*
3. *What did God promise Elijah and the woman?*
4. *Did God keep His promise?*

WHAT DO YOU SEE?

What do you see in this house? What would you not find in your house?

124

A Boy Comes Back to Life

1 Kings 17—24

This woman was crying a few minutes ago. Her son had died. She was sad. She thought God was punishing her. She thought she would never see her son alive again. Then the poor woman talked to Elijah. She knew Elijah did special work for God. Elijah talked to God. He asked God to help. "Let this boy come back to life again," he prayed. What do you think happened next? The boy began to breathe. He was alive again. Now you know why the boy and his mother look so happy. Now you know why Elijah looks happy too.

A TIME TO SHARE
1. *Why do these people look so happy?*
2. *Who brought this boy back to life?*
3. *Can an ordinary person bring someone back to life?*
4. *Who can?*

Elijah Prays for Fire

1 Kings 18

"The Lord is God!" says Elijah. He is God's friend.

"Baal is the true god," says King Ahab. But Baal is only a statue. The king thinks this statue sends rain. He thinks people should worship Baal.

"Come to Mount Carmel," Elijah tells the king. "Bring the prophets of Baal." When they come, Elijah tells the prophets of Baal to make an altar. They ask Baal to send fire down to the altar. But how can a statue do that? Then Elijah makes an altar. He asks God to send fire down to his altar. God sends a big fire. It burns the altar and the meat on it. It even burns up the water around it. Baal could not send fire. But God did. "The Lord is the true God!" the people said. He is, isn't He?

A TIME TO SHARE
1. *What is Elijah doing?*
2. *What is he asking God to do?*
3. *Why did God send the fire?*
4. *Who should we worship and obey?*

WHAT DO YOU SEE?

A fire is burning. Did Baal send it? Who did? What is this fire burning up?

God Whispers to Elijah

1 Kings 19:1-18

Elijah has run away from his home. The queen wants to kill him. Elijah is hiding here on this big mountain. He thinks people back home are not listening to him. He wants God to do something big to show that He is God. Suddenly the wind blows. It is a terrible wind. "God must be in that wind!" Elijah thinks. But He isn't. Then an earthquake shakes the mountain. "God must be in that earthquake!" Elijah thinks. But He isn't. A big fire roars on the mountain. "God must be in that big fire!" Elijah thinks. But He isn't. Shhhh! Do you hear Someone whisper? Elijah does. God is whispering to him. God does not need big things to show people He is God. What God says is important, even when He whispers!

A TIME TO SHARE
1. *Who is talking to Elijah?*
2. *Is God talking in a big voice or a whisper?*
3. *What Book tells us what God says?*

WHAT DO YOU SEE?

What tells you that the wind is blowing? What tells you there is an earthquake? Point to the fire. Is God in these things?

WHAT DO YOU SEE?
Do you think this is a good vineyard? How can you tell?

Naboth's Vineyard

1 Kings 21

Look at King Ahab's beautiful robes. He looks like a rich man, doesn't he? Ahab was not only rich, but very, very selfish. He wanted a beautiful vineyard near his palace. But Naboth owned the vineyard. It was all Naboth had. He would not sell it. When the wicked queen heard that her husband, the king, wanted the vineyard, she had some men kill Naboth. Then she gave the vineyard to King Ahab. Ahab is pleased as he comes to look at his vineyard. But look who has come to see him—Elijah. "God will punish you!" Elijah tells the king. Now the king is sorry. Most of us are sorry when we know we will be punished, aren't we?

A TIME TO SHARE
1. *What is Elijah telling the king?*
2. *Why will the king be punished?*
3. *Are we punished for good or for bad things?*
4. *How can you keep from getting punished?*

A Story of Two Kings

1 Kings 22:1-40

Here are two kings on their thrones. One is Ahab. The other is Jehoshaphat. That is a big name even for a king. These two kings want to lead their armies in a battle. They think it is all right. "But does the Lord think it is?" Jehoshaphat asks. He is a good king. He should not be here helping bad King Ahab. King Ahab calls for some men who pretend they are God's prophets. They lie to the two kings. They say the kings will win. "That's not true!" Micaiah says. Do you see him? He is God's prophet. The kings should listen to him. But they don't. "King Ahab will be killed," Micaiah warns. That is just what happened. We should listen to people like Micaiah, shouldn't we?

A TIME TO SHARE
1. *Which man is Micaiah?*
2. *What is he telling the two kings?*
3. *Will they listen to him?*
4. *Do you listen to your parents and teachers?*

WHAT DO YOU SEE?

How would you feel if you were Ahab? Would you stay at home? Would you listen to God's prophet?

Elisha Does God's Work

2 Kings 2:1-18

Elijah was God's helper. He did many wonderful things for God. But now it was time for him to go to heaven. Who would do Elijah's work then? "I will," said Elisha. Now do you see what is happening to Elijah? He is going up into heaven. God sends a whirlwind to take him. Elisha is holding Elijah's coat. He knows now that he will do Elijah's work. He will be God's special helper too.

A TIME TO SHARE

1. *Which man is Elisha?*
2. *What will he do now?*
3. *What can you do to help God?*

WHAT DO YOU SEE?

Can you find the horses and chariot of fire? God sent those. They are helping Elijah go into heaven. Can you find Elijah's coat? Elisha is holding it. Elisha will keep that coat. He will use it to do God's work.

Pots of Oil

2 Kings 4:1-7

This poor woman was in trouble. She owed a
lot of money to a man. But she could not pay
him. "I will take your boys," the man told her.
"I will sell them. They will be slaves." The poor
woman was afraid. She ran to see Elisha. Elisha told her to borrow jars and pots from her
neighbors. "God will help you," he said. "Pour
oil from your little jar. Keep pouring it into the
pots. As long as you keep pouring, the oil will
fill these pots." The woman believed Elisha.
She believed God. She did exactly what Elisha
said. Do you see what is happening? God is
doing what He said He would do. God always
keeps His promises.

A TIME TO SHARE
1. *What did Elisha tell the woman to do?*
2. *What did the woman do?*
3. *Do you try to do what God wants you to do?*

WHAT DO YOU SEE?
How many jars and pots do you see? What is in them?
How did all this oil get in these pots?

WHAT DO YOU SEE?

Look at the room in this house. How is it different from
your room? How would you like to live here?

A Happy Family

2 Kings 4:18-37

This looks like a happy family, doesn't it? But these people were not happy awhile ago. That little boy was dead. He had been in the field working. But suddenly his head hurt very much. His mother held him, but the boy died. Think how sad this woman was when she saw her boy dead. But she didn't sit there crying. She went to find Elisha. "Help me!" she begged. Elisha hurried to her house. He went into the room where the dead boy was. Then he prayed. "Lord, help us," he begged. The boy sneezed. He was alive! Now look how happy everyone is. You would be happy too if God did something special for you.

A TIME TO SHARE

1. Which man is Elisha?

2. Who are these other people?

3. What special thing did God do for them?

4. Have you thanked God for special things?

WHAT DO YOU SEE?

Do you think Naaman and his wife are rich or poor? Why
do you think this?

Naaman Obeys

2 Kings 5:1-14

Naaman was a general. He told many soldiers what to do. "Go here!" Naaman said. The soldiers went. "Do this!" Naaman said. The soldiers did it. But Naaman was in trouble. He had a terrible disease. It was called leprosy. No doctor could help him. "I know someone who can help you," a little girl said. She told Naaman about Elisha. Naaman hurried to see Elisha. "Wash seven times in the Jordan River," Elisha told Naaman. Naaman did not want to do that. But he did. Now look at him! God made him well. Naaman is happy. His wife is happy. The little girl who told him about Elisha is happy.

A TIME TO SHARE
1. *Why does Naaman look happy?*
2. *What did he do?*
3. *Are you happier when you obey or disobey?*

An Army of Angels

2 Kings 6:8-17

What would you think if you saw a big army of angels? What would you think if they were there to help you? Do you see an army of angels? They have horses and chariots. They are there to help Elisha if he needs them. But at first the young man did not see them. Then Elisha asked God to let the young man see them. Think how excited this young man is. He should be! Not many of us see an army of angels, do we?

A TIME TO SHARE
1. *What is that on the hill outside town?*
2. *What is this angel army doing there?*
3. *Name three ways God helps you.*

142

WHAT DO YOU SEE?

Point to five things you do not see in your house. What do
these things tell you about Elisha and the way he lived?

Helping People Who Hurt Us

2 Kings 6:18-23

This is Elisha, leading a soldier. The soldier is blind. So are all the other soldiers behind him. God made these men blind. They came to hurt Elisha. Now they can't see. Someone must help them. Elisha could hurt them. He could have them killed. But he will not do that. Elisha is helping people who wanted to hurt him. Soon God will make them see again. Then they will be sorry they tried to hurt Elisha.

A TIME TO SHARE

1. *What did these men want to do to Elisha?*

2. *Is Elisha helping them or hurting them?*

3. *Does someone want to hurt you?*

4. *Should you try to help or hurt that person?*

WHAT DO YOU SEE?

Do you think these men are soldiers? What do you see
that shows they are soldiers?

WHAT DO YOU SEE?

The man holding the crown is a priest. He hid Joash until he was seven years old. Look at the priest's clothes. That's what he was supposed to wear. The building where they are standing is the temple. It is God's house.

The Boy Who Became King

2 Kings 11

These people were not very happy. A wicked queen ruled them. She hurt them. She tried to kill this boy, named Joash, and his family. But she could not find him. The old priest hid Joash. Now he is seven years old. Now the people are making him king. The wicked queen will not rule them anymore. The people are happy now. It is much better to have a good king or queen than a bad one.

A TIME TO SHARE
1. *What is happening here?*
2. *What would you think if you were this boy?*
3. *Would you ask God to help you?*

Giving for God's House

2 Kings 12:1-16

For a long time people did not fix God's house. They did not clean it. Now it is dirty and broken down. King Joash does not like that. He wants God's house to be beautiful again. "Get some money. Fix God's house," the king tells the priests. So the priests put this chest near the door of God's house. Now look what is happening. These people are giving money. They want to fix God's house too. Wouldn't you want to give some money if you were here?

A TIME TO SHARE
1. *What are the people putting into the chest?*
2. *Why are they doing this?*
3. *Do you like to give money at God's house?*
4. *Do you like to make God's house clean?*

WHAT DO YOU SEE?

Do you see some children? Point to them. Do you see
some mothers? Who else do you see?

God Helps Hezekiah

2 Kings 19

This man does not look like a king. But he is.
This is a good king called Hezekiah. But he is
in trouble. Thousands of soldiers have come
into his land. They want to take his land from
him. Hezekiah does not have enough soldiers
to fight. So what can he do? Who can help him?
Hezekiah knows. God can help him. He goes to
God's house. He takes a letter from the enemy.
Hezekiah spreads the letter on the floor. Then
he prays. He asks God to help him. Do you
know what happens next? God sends an angel
to fight those thousands of soldiers. Now Hezekiah knows that God is stronger than an army.
Remember that when you pray!

A TIME TO SHARE
1. *What is King Hezekiah doing?*
2. *How will God help him?*
3. *When you need help, do you ask God?*

150

WHAT DO YOU SEE?

Look how this king is dressed. This is called sackcloth. It is very rough cloth. People put it on to show God they were sad and wanted His help. Look at the room. This is the temple, God's house.

God's Word Is Found

2 Kings 22:1—23:3

The man sitting on the throne is Josiah. He wants to be a good king. He does not want to be like his father, bad King Amon. King Amon did not care about God. So God's house became dirty and broken down. People lost the only copy of God's Word. "Fix God's house!" King Josiah ordered. People began to fix God's house. One day they found something rolled up. It was God's Word. A man is reading it now to King Josiah. But King Josiah is sad. "We have not been doing what God wants," said Josiah. The king told the people to come to God's house. Then he read God's Word to them. "Obey the Lord!" the king told the people. "We will!" the people promised.

A TIME TO SHARE
1. *What kind of king was Josiah?*
2. *What did he tell the people to do?*
3. *Do you want to do what God says?*

WHAT DO YOU SEE?

Do you see the man reading God's Word? He is reading
from a scroll. God's Word was written on this scroll. See
how it is rolled up on rollers?

WHAT DO YOU SEE?

Do you see the tents? These people stayed here for three days. They would not hurry on their trip. They wanted to be sure that God was with them.

154

God Goes with His People

Ezra 7—8

These people are going on a long trip. They do not have cars, or trains, or airplanes. They must walk all the way on trails with rocks. The sun will be hot. Robbers may try to steal from them or hurt them. But look! What are they doing? They are asking God to go with them on this trip. "God will take care of us," Ezra tells the people. Ezra kneels down by the river. All the people stop. Ezra asks God to go with them. Do you think He will?

A TIME TO SHARE
1. *What are these people doing?*
2. *Do you ask God to go with you on your trips?*
3. *Will you remember to do that next time?*

WHAT DO YOU SEE?

Do these men look sad or happy? Do they look like they are talking about something important? Why do you say that?

Nehemiah Prays

Nehemiah 1:1—2:10

Shhh! Nehemiah is praying. He is sad because he has heard some bad news. The men with him have come from Jerusalem. Nehemiah's family lived there many years ago. "The walls are broken down," the men told Nehemiah. "The city is a mess." This made Nehemiah sad. That is why he is praying. He is asking God to let him go to Jerusalem. He is asking God to let him build the walls there. Nehemiah loves the country where his family lived. He wants to pray for it. He wants to do something to help.

A TIME TO SHARE
1. *What is Nehemiah doing?*
2. *What does he want God to do for him?*
3. *Do you ever pray for your country?*

Building a Wall

Nehemiah 2:17—7:3

Building a wall is hard work. Look at Nehemiah and his friends working! They are glad to do this. They love their city, Jerusalem. They want it to have a strong wall. This wall will keep enemies out. But the enemies do not like the wall. They do not like Nehemiah and his friends. The enemies want to hurt the people. Then the people will have to stop building the wall. "Don't be afraid," Nehemiah tells his friends. "God is great. He will help us." Nehemiah was right. God helped Nehemiah and his friends. He helped them build the wall.

A TIME TO SHARE
1. *What are Nehemiah and his friends doing?*
2. *Who is helping them?*
3. *Do you want God to help you today?*

WHAT DO YOU SEE?

Can you guess what each man is doing? Have you ever
seen tools like these?

Ezra Reads God's Word

Nehemiah 8:1-12

Ezra is reading from God's Word. This does not look much like your Bible. But it is the part of the Bible that Ezra had. Ezra reads. Then he tells what it means. He tells the people what God wants them to do. Some people begin to cry. They are sad because they have not done what God wants. "Don't cry," Ezra tells them. "This is a happy day. Go home and thank God for what He has given you." That's good for us to remember, isn't it? Sometimes we are sorry for what we haven't done. That's a good time to thank God for what He has done.

A TIME TO SHARE
1. *What is Ezra reading?*
2. *Why are some people sad?*
3. *Are you happy when you please God?*
4. *Are you happy when you please your parents?*

WHAT DO YOU SEE?

Think about the time when your minister reads God's Word to the church. What is different here?

This Queen Is Brave

Esther 2—8

Queen Esther is not supposed to come to see the king. That's a rule in this land. The rule says that the king can kill her for coming to him. Why did Esther do this? She has something important to tell the king. She can't wait. But look! The king is holding out a golden rod, called a scepter. Esther knows that when the king does this, she can talk. She will tell the king a secret. "A man wants to hurt my family and friends," Esther tells the king. The king will not let that wicked man hurt Queen Esther's family and friends. He will help her. Now Esther is glad that she came. She must have been afraid. But she came to see the king anyway!

A TIME TO SHARE
1. *Why did Queen Esther come here?*
2. *Was she brave to do this? Why?*
3. *Do you want to do things that you should do?*
4. *Will you do them even when you are afraid?*

WHAT DO YOU SEE?

What colors do you see in this room? Point to some of them.

Isaiah Obeys God

Isaiah 6

You know this man is praying, don't you? This is Isaiah. Today something happens while he is praying. He sees a bright light. He sees God sitting on His throne in heaven. Angels sing "Holy, holy, holy is the Lord." What would you think if you saw all these things? Would you be afraid? Isaiah was afraid too. Here he is on his knees. He asks God to forgive any bad thing he has done. God forgives Isaiah. He asks Isaiah to do some special work for Him. Isaiah wrote part of our Bible. That part is called Isaiah. God helped Isaiah write it. Aren't you glad Isaiah did what God wanted?

A TIME TO SHARE
1. *What does Isaiah see?*
2. *What does God want him to do?*
3. *Would you like to listen to Isaiah?*
4. *Ask someone to read Isaiah 53:3-10.*

164

WHAT DO YOU SEE?

Isaiah is kneeling in the temple, God's house. Do you see the bright light? Isaiah is telling God that he will do what God wants. Isaiah lived hundred of years before Jesus came. But he wrote about Jesus. He told how Jesus would be our Saviour. Isaiah 53:3-10 is about Jesus.

165

WHAT DO YOU SEE?

Do you see the fire? Homes and palaces in Jeremiah's time did not have furnaces. This was one way to heat a room. This was something like the grill where you cook hamburgers.

Jeremiah Listens and Obeys

Jeremiah 36

Do you see the rolled-up paper? It is called a scroll. God told Jeremiah exactly what to say on that scroll. But the king does not like what he hears. He is a bad king. He does not want God to tell him what to do. So the king cuts the scroll into pieces. Look! He is burning each piece as he cuts it. But the king cannot stop God! God tells Jeremiah what to say on another scroll. The king does not burn this one. Now you may read what God said. It is in your Bible. It is a part called Jeremiah. Aren't you glad Jeremiah listened to God? Aren't you glad he did exactly what God told him to do?

A TIME TO SHARE
1. *What is the king doing?*
2. *Why is he burning the scroll?*
3. *Aren't you glad Jeremiah did what God said?*
4. *Aren't you glad when you do what God says?*

Daniel Says No Thank You

Daniel 1

A servant brings some food. It is the same kind of food that the king eats. It is the richest food in the land. But Daniel and his friends do not want to eat it. God does not want them to eat the king's rich food. He does not want them to drink the king's wine. So they say no thank you. Do you say no thank you to things that don't please God?

A TIME TO SHARE

1. Why didn't Daniel want to eat the food?

2. What did he say?

3. What should you say to bad things?

WHAT DO YOU SEE?

Point to the different bowls and dishes with food. Do you
see the man bringing the food? Which persons are Daniel
and his friends?

WHAT DO YOU SEE?

Look on the ground. Do you see some men lying there?
The furnace was so hot that they died. Now look at Daniel's friends. How can they stand there like that?

Daniel's Three Friends

Daniel 3

You can't see the big golden statue here. The king put it in a field. Then he told everyone to bow down to the statue. People should not do that, should they? Daniel's three friends would not do it. They thought they should bow down to God, not to a statue. The king was angry. Most kings get angry when people will not do what the king says. The king told his men to throw Daniel's friends into a big furnace. Do you see them standing in it? Do you see Someone else there with them? The king was afraid. He saw that the fire could not hurt the men. How could Daniel's three friends stand in a hot furnace? Who was this other Person? "He looks like the Son of God!" the king cried out. God took special care of these men, didn't He?

A TIME TO SHARE
1. *Why did the king put Daniel's friends here?*
2. *Who came to help them?*
3. *Do you ask God to help you each day?*

WHAT DO YOU SEE?

A big party was going on here. Do you see some things that tell you it was a party? Point to them. Do you see Daniel?

172

God Writes to a King

Daniel 5

The king is afraid. He should be! A giant hand wrote those words on the wall. The king does not know what they say. Not one of his friends can tell him. But Daniel is telling him! He is telling the king that God is not pleased with him. God will not let him be king anymore.

A TIME TO SHARE
1. *What is Daniel telling the king?*
2. *Do you think the king is afraid?*
3. *What would you think if you were the king?*
4. *What should he do now? What would you do?*

Daniel in the Lions' Den

Daniel 6

What is Daniel doing with these lions? They may not look fierce, but they are. They eat people. But these lions cannot eat Daniel. Do you know why? God has shut their mouths. God is keeping Daniel safe from some wicked men. These men do not like Daniel. They want to kill him. They tricked the king so that he would make a law. "Stop praying," this law said. Daniel would not stop praying. "If you don't stop praying, you will be put into a den of lions," the law said. Daniel would not stop praying. So Daniel was put into this den of lions. Aren't you glad God shut the lions' mouths? Aren't you glad God protected Daniel?

A TIME TO SHARE
1. *Why was Daniel put into this lions' den?*
2. *Who is keeping Daniel from getting hurt?*
3. *Have you asked God to keep you safe today?*

WHAT DO YOU SEE?

How many lions do you see? Look at their mouths. Can
you see their teeth? Why not?

Jonah Runs Away

Jonah 1—3

Jonah is trying to run away. He thinks he can run away from God. But he can't, can he? Poor Jonah! He should know that God is everywhere. Nobody can run away from God. Do you see Jonah ready to get on this ship? God told Jonah to go to a bad city called Nineveh. Those people needed someone to tell them about God. Then they could stop being bad. They could ask God to help them. But Jonah does not want to go to Nineveh. He wants these people to be punished. That's why Jonah is running away from God. Do you remember what happened to Jonah? A big fish swallowed him. Then the fish spit up Jonah. Now Jonah knew he should not try to run from God. Jonah knew he should do exactly what God told him.

A TIME TO SHARE
1. *What did God want Jonah to do?*
2. *What is Jonah trying to do?*
3. *Can you ever run away from God? Why not?*

WHAT DO YOU SEE?

Point to some different things on the ship. Do you see the money? People paid this money to ride on the ship. The rolls of paper were books. Point to the sails on the ship. What do they tell you about this ship?

An Angel Brings Good News

Luke 1:26-38

This beautiful woman is Mary. But do you see who is with her? This is an angel! God sent this angel to talk to Mary. The angel has some good news. "The Lord has chosen you," the angel is telling Mary. "You will be the mother of God's Son. You will call Him Jesus." What can Mary say? She is so happy that she will be Jesus' mother. Jesus is our Saviour. He was punished for the bad things we have done. God sent Him to do this. Wouldn't any good woman want to be Jesus' mother?

A TIME TO SHARE
1. *What did the angel tell Mary?*
2. *Do you think Mary is happy with this news?*
3. *Do you like to hear good news?*
4. *Do you like God's Good News in the Bible?*

WHAT DO YOU SEE?
Which one is the angel? Which one is Mary? Don't you
think Mary is beautiful?

Mary Visits Elizabeth

Luke 1:39-56

Mary has a secret. She wants to tell her cousin Elizabeth. But Elizabeth already knows. God has told her. "Mary, you are going to have a baby," Elizabeth says. "He will be God's Son." Elizabeth has a secret too. She wants to tell her cousin Mary. But Mary already knows. God has told her that Elizabeth will have a baby too. He is a special baby. Her baby will grow up to be a preacher. Mary is staying with Elizabeth for three months. Think of the fun they are having, talking about their babies!

A TIME TO SHARE
1. *How long did Mary stay with Elizabeth?*
2. *What did these two ladies talk about?*
3. *What would you like to ask Mary?*

WHAT DO YOU SEE?

What do you think Elizabeth is saying to Mary now?
How is this house different from yours?

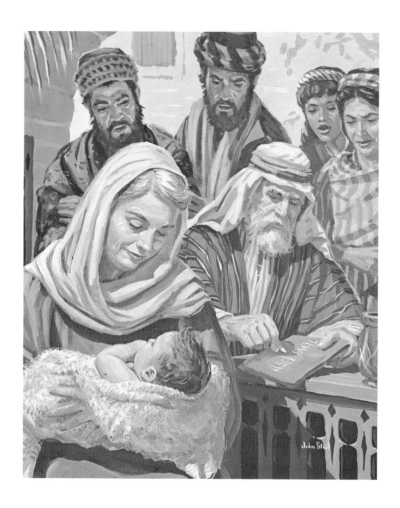

WHAT DO YOU SEE?

What is that in Zacharias' hands? He is holding a tablet.
It is not made of paper. It is wood, covered with wax.
Zacharias scratches John's name on the tablet.

John Is Born

Luke 1:57-80

Do you remember this lady? She is Elizabeth, Mary's cousin. Now look what she has in her arms! There is her baby boy. But what will she and her husband Zacharias name him? The friends and neighbors think the parents will name him Zacharias. He would be named for his father. But do you see the baby's father writing? He is writing the baby's name. "His name is John," Zacharias writes. That's the name God wants him to have.

A TIME TO SHARE
1. *Why did Zacharias name the baby John?*
2. *Do you like to do what God wants you to do?*

Baby Jesus Is Born

Luke 2:1-7

Mary and Joseph are in a stable. This is a room where cows and sheep and donkeys stay. It is the room where the Baby Jesus was born. Do you see Mary holding Him? She is the Baby Jesus' mother. But God is His Father. God wants Joseph to take care of Jesus. Would you like to say something to Baby Jesus?

A TIME TO SHARE
1. *Where was Baby Jesus born?*
2. *Who is holding Him?*
3. *What will Joseph do?*

WHAT DO YOU SEE?

How do you know this is a stable? What do you see?

WHAT DO YOU SEE?

Do you see the fire? Why do you think the shepherds
have made a fire? Do you see the sheep? Point to them.
Can you find a sixth shepherd?

186

Angels Appear to Shepherds

Luke 2:8-14

These shepherds are looking at something strange. Do you see it? It is a bright light. But they see something you don't see. An angel is talking to them. "Don't be afraid," the angel says. "I have good news for you! The Saviour was born tonight. He is lying in a manger in Bethlehem." Now look at the shepherds' faces. Do you know what they see? Thousands and thousands of angels are in the sky. That's why there is such a bright light. These angels are like a choir. "Glory to God in heaven!" the angels say. We don't know if they are singing or saying it together. But wouldn't you like to be there with the shepherds?

A TIME TO SHARE

1. *What do these shepherds see?*
2. *What are the angels saying?*
3. *What would you like to ask these shepherds?*

187

WHAT DO YOU SEE?

What has the young shepherd brought? Would you like to hold this little lamb? Do you see the stars? Is this daytime or nighttime? Why is there hay near Baby Jesus?

Shepherds Visit Baby Jesus

Luke 2:15-20

The shepherds are not with their sheep now. Someone else is taking care of their sheep. Here they are in Bethlehem. They are so happy to see this Baby. Do you remember what the angel said? This Baby is the Saviour. He is Baby Jesus! Mary and Joseph are glad to show the Baby Jesus to the shepherds. The shepherds are glad they can see this special Baby.

A TIME TO SHARE
1. *Who told these shepherds about Baby Jesus?*
2. *Where are these people?*
3. *What would you do if you were here?*

Simeon Holds Baby Jesus

Luke 2:21-38

This man holding Baby Jesus looks happy, doesn't he? He is happy! Long ago God told Simeon that he would see the Saviour. Simeon waited and waited and waited. Now today Mary and Joseph have come to God's house with Baby Jesus. God told Simeon to come here too. He told Simeon that this Baby is the Saviour. Anna has come to see Baby Jesus too. She loves God. How excited she is to see Baby Jesus. She knows that He is the Saviour. God told her. She will tell many others that Jesus has come. She will tell them that He is the Saviour. We should each do that, shouldn't we?

A TIME TO SHARE
1. *Who is holding Baby Jesus?*
2. *Why does he look happy?*
3. *What will Anna do?*
4. *Do you know that Jesus is the Saviour?*

WHAT DO YOU SEE?

Look at the way these people dress. Point to some things that you and your family do not wear.

Wise Men Follow a Star

Matthew 2:1-8

Look at that bright star in the sky. These three men are following it. They are called wise men. They know that Baby Jesus is born. The star will lead them to King Herod. Then it will lead them to Baby Jesus. They have some special gifts for Him!

A TIME TO SHARE

1. *Where are these three men going?*

2. *What is the star doing?*

3. *What would you like to ask these men?*

WHAT DO YOU SEE?

The wise men are riding camels. They will travel many miles on their camels. It is better than walking. But aren't you glad you don't go on trips that way?

Wise Men Give Jesus Gifts

Matthew 2:9-12

Here are the wise men again. They followed the star. It showed them how to find Jesus. These men have come on a long trip. They have some beautiful gifts for Jesus. Do you see what they have brought? They have spices called myrrh and frankincense. These spices cost a lot of money. They also have gold. After the wise men give Jesus their gifts, they will bow down. They will worship Him. They know that He is God's Son, the Saviour.

A TIME TO SHARE
1. *Are these good gifts?*
2. *What will the wise men do next?*
3. *Do you like to give Jesus good gifts?*

WHAT DO YOU SEE?

Point to each gift the wise men brought. Can you name
the three kinds of gifts?

Mary and Joseph Go to Egypt

Matthew 2:13-18

Joseph and Mary are in a hurry. The wicked king wants to kill Jesus. God told Joseph to take Jesus to Egypt. Now they are on their way. Mary is riding the donkey. She is holding Jesus. God promised them that He would take care of them. He promised that He would take care of Jesus. You know God will keep His promise, don't you?

A TIME TO SHARE

1. *Where are these people going?*
2. *Why are Mary and Joseph taking Jesus there?*
3. *Do you think God keeps every promise?*

WHAT DO YOU SEE?

Look at the road. When you take a trip, what kind of roads do you go on? Do they look like this road? Roads in Bible times were like paths. Donkeys and camels walked on them. People walked on them. But there were no cars.

WHAT DO YOU SEE?

Do you see the stone fences? Do you see the houses? How do they look different from your house?

Coming Home to Nazareth

Matthew 2:19-23

A wicked king wanted to kill Jesus. But that king is dead now. It is safe for Mary and Joseph to bring Jesus back home. Do you see them traveling? They have been in Egypt. It is far away from home. Now they are back home in Nazareth. It has been a long time since they have been here. They are so glad to be home. Aren't you glad when you come home from a long trip?

A TIME TO SHARE

1. *Where have these people been?*
2. *Do you think God is going with them?*
3. *Do you ask God to go with you on a trip?*

WHAT DO YOU SEE?

How many tools can you find? Point to each one. Can you find Joseph?

200

Jesus Helps Joseph

Luke 2:39-40

Look at Jesus pounding with His hammer. He is helping Joseph. This is a carpenter's shop. Joseph makes things from wood. Jesus is old enough to be Joseph's helper. Jesus wants to be a helper. Aren't you glad Jesus showed us how to be good helpers?

A TIME TO SHARE
1. *What is Jesus doing here?*
2. *Who is He helping?*
3. *Do you like to be a helper?*

WHAT DO YOU SEE?

How many men do you see with Jesus? Are they young men or older men? They are in God's house. It is called the temple.

The Boy Jesus Obeys

Luke 2:41-52

The Boy here is Jesus. He is 12 now. But who are all these men around Him? They are important teachers. They are very wise men. They know more than most men. But they are surprised today. This 12-year-old Boy is teaching them! He is telling them about God. They wonder how He knows so much about God. If only they knew that Jesus is God's Son! Soon Mary and Joseph come. They tell Jesus it is time to go home. Then Jesus obeys them and goes home with them. Jesus showed us how to obey, didn't He?

A TIME TO SHARE
1. *How old is Jesus?*
2. *What is He doing here?*
3. *What will He do when Mary and Joseph come?*
4. *Do you obey your parents without grumbling?*

John Tells about Jesus

Matthew 3:1-12

Does that man with the stick look like your preacher? Do the other people look like your friends and neighbors at church? This man is John. Sometimes he is called John the Baptist. He is preaching to these people. He does not have a pulpit. This is not a church. But the people have come to listen. "Stop doing bad things," John tells them. "The Saviour has come! God sent me to tell you about Him." John tells these people about Jesus. Don't you think they should listen to him?

A TIME TO SHARE
1. *What is John doing?*
2. *Why should these people listen?*
3. *Do you listen when people tell about Jesus?*

WHAT DO YOU SEE?

Do you see the soldier? He has come here to listen to John. Point to the cloak John is wearing. It is made of camels' hair.

Jesus Is Baptized

Matthew 3:13-17

Do you see John standing in the river? Do you remember him? He preached to many people. He told them to be sorry for the bad things they did. Then he told them to get ready to receive Jesus. Many who heard John were sorry for the bad things they did. John baptized these people in this river. Today John is surprised. Jesus asks John to baptize Him too. When he does God's Spirit comes down like a dove. "This is My Son!" God says. "I am pleased with Him." We want God to say He is pleased with us, don't we?

A TIME TO SHARE
1. *What has just happened here?*
2. *What did God say about Jesus?*
3. *Do you want God to be pleased with you?*
4. *What are some things you should do?*

WHAT DO YOU SEE?

Where is the dove? It is not really a dove, is it? It is God's Spirit coming down from heaven.

Jesus Is Tempted

Matthew 4:1-11

How many people do you see with Jesus? It looks like He is all alone. But He isn't! Satan is there. He is talking to Jesus. He wants Jesus to do some bad things. Satan wants us to do bad things too, doesn't he? But Jesus is saying no. He keeps on telling Satan words from the Bible. Satan doesn't like that. He does not like to hear us say no. He does not like to hear us say words from the Bible. Remember that when Satan tempts you to do something bad.

A TIME TO SHARE

1. *What does Satan want Jesus to do here?*
2. *What does Satan want you to do?*
3. *What did Jesus do?*
4. *What should you do?*

WHAT DO YOU SEE?
Does this look like a rich beautiful land? Does it look
like a desert? What makes you think this?

209

Jesus in God's House

John 2:13-16

This is God's house, the temple. But it doesn't look like it! Some men are selling sheep and birds and cattle. They are not doing this to help God's house. They are cheating the people who come to buy. Wouldn't you be angry if this happened in your church? Jesus is angry. Look at Him! He is knocking a table over. Do you see the money spilling? "Get out of here!" Jesus tells these men. "This is God's house. People should pray here. But you are stealing from people!" Do you know what these men did? They got out!

A TIME TO SHARE
1. *What is Jesus doing?*
2. *Why is He angry?*
3. *Do you help keep God's house quiet?*
4. *Do you help keep God's house beautiful?*

WHAT DO YOU SEE?

Point to some of the tables and chairs. Which are knocked over? What else do you see?

Jesus Talks to Nicodemus

John 3

Do you see the man talking to Jesus? He is an important man. People think he knows a lot about God. This man Nicodemus thought he knew a lot about God too. Then he heard Jesus talk. Jesus said things about God that Nicodemus did not know. Now he has come to see Jesus. It is night. The stars are shining. The wind is blowing softly. He listens carefully as Jesus talks. "You must be born again, Nicodemus," Jesus says. Then He says, "I am God's Son." Nicodemus can be a new person if he believes in Jesus. You can too!

A TIME TO SHARE
1. *What do you know about Nicodemus?*
2. *What did Jesus tell him?*
3. *What would you like Jesus to do for you?*

WHAT DO YOU SEE?

Where are Jesus and Nicodemus? This is a flat roof of a house. Do you see the other houses? Look at the flat roofs. People often went up on these flat roofs to talk or sleep.

WHAT DO YOU SEE?

Do you think this father and his son love each other?
Why do you think that? Do you think they are both
happy? Why do you think that?

Jesus Heals a Boy

John 4:43-54

"Please help me!" a rich man asked Jesus. "My son is very sick." This man wanted Jesus to come home with him. He wanted Jesus to heal his son. "Go home," Jesus told the man. "Your son is all right." The man looked at Jesus. He believed Him. He hurried home, which was far away. What do you think he found? His son is well! Now look how happy the father is. Look how happy his boy is too. It is good to believe exactly what Jesus says.

A TIME TO SHARE

1. *What did this man want Jesus to do?*
2. *How did Jesus heal this boy?*
3. *How do you know the man believed in Jesus?*
4. *Do you ask Jesus to do important things?*

Jesus Reads God's Word

Luke 4:16-30

Would you like to hear Jesus read God's Word? Would you like to hear Him preach? Of course you would. Jesus is reading God's Word to these men. He is preaching to them. But they are angry. They do not like what He is saying. He is telling them that He is God's Son. They think He is only a neighbor there in Nazareth. They think He is only a carpenter. Don't you think they should listen carefully to Jesus? Don't you think they should believe what He says?

A TIME TO SHARE
1. *What is Jesus doing?*
2. *Why are these men angry?*
3. *Do you think they should believe Him?*
4. *Do you believe what Jesus says?*

WHAT DO YOU SEE?

Jesus is reading and preaching in a synagogue. It is God's house in Nazareth. What do you see that you do not find at your church?

Jesus Helps Peter Fish

Luke 5:1-11

Look at those fish! They are jumping in the nets. They are jumping out of the nets. Peter and his friends are surprised. They fished all night. But they did not catch one fish. Now where did all these fish come from? Jesus knows. He told them where to put their nets. How did He know? Jesus is God's Son. He knows everything.

A TIME TO SHARE
1. *Why were Peter and his friends surprised?*
2. *How did Jesus know where to fish?*
3. *Do you want Jesus to help you do something?*

WHAT DO YOU SEE?

How many boats do you see? How many fishermen?
These men work together catching fish. They are Jesus'
friends. Later they will stop catching fish. They will be
Jesus' helpers.

Four Friends Follow Jesus

Matthew 4:18-22

Here comes Jesus. He is waving to His friends. There are four friends; Peter, Andrew, James, and John. You see only two here. These friends are mending their nets. They catch fish with these nets. They sell the fish. That is the way they make money. "Come with Me," Jesus tells His friends. "Be My helpers." Do you know what these friends will do? They will leave their nets. They will leave their boats. They will stop fishing. They will go with Jesus. From now on they will help Jesus do His work.

A TIME TO SHARE
1. *What are these friends doing?*
2. *What did Jesus ask them to do?*
3. *Do you think they will like helping Jesus?*
4. *Would you like to help Jesus?*

WHAT DO YOU SEE?

Do you see the nets? Do you see the boat? There is a sail
on the boat. Do you know what that sail did? The men
opened the sail. Then the wind blew the boat across the
water.

WHAT DO YOU SEE?

Can you find a bed? What else do you see in this house?
Do you see the stairs? Do you see a window?

Jesus Heals a Woman

Mark 1:29-34

Peter and his wife look happy, don't they? They should be. That's Peter's mother-in-law in the center. A few minutes before she was sick. Now look at her! She is ready to get up and help in the kitchen. Do you know what happened? Jesus touched her hand. Suddenly her fever was gone. She was well! Jesus can do wonderful things, can't He? That's because He is God's Son.

A TIME TO SHARE
1. *Why do Peter and his wife look happy?*
2. *What did Jesus do here?*
3. *Are you glad Jesus can do wonderful things?*
4. *Do you ask Him to help you?*

WHAT DO YOU SEE?

Do you see some crutches? What else do you see that shows these people are sick? Is this in town or in the country? How do you know?

Jesus Heals Many People

Luke 4:40-44

Most of these people are sick or crippled. But who can help them? There are a few doctors, but these doctors do not know how to heal the people. They do not have good medicine. They do not know what doctors today know. There are no hospitals. There are no nurses. These poor people need help! They need Jesus. He is God's Son. He can heal them. Do you think that is what Jesus is doing?

A TIME TO SHARE

1. *Why did these people come to Jesus?*
2. *Is He helping them? What is He doing?*
3. *Will Jesus help you if you ask Him?*

Jesus Heals a Man

Luke 5:17-26

Look! There is a hole in the roof. Four of those men standing there made that hole. A friend was sick. They couldn't get inside this house to see Jesus. They thought Jesus could heal their friend. So they took off part of the roof. Then they let their friend down into the room. Jesus must have smiled when He saw the man coming through the roof. Then He healed the man. Now do you see him? The man is well. He is rolling up his mat-bed. He will carry it home. Don't you think this man will thank God on the way home? He did!

A TIME TO SHARE
1. *Who brought this man here?*
2. *How did they get him into the room?*
3. *Did the man thank God?*
4. *Should you remember to thank God too?*

WHAT DO YOU SEE?

Do you see the rope? What did some men do with this rope? Where is the mat-bed? This is probably the only bed this man has. Mat-beds were something like sleeping bags.

Jesus Talks to Matthew

Luke 5:27-28

People did not like Matthew. He made them pay taxes. Sometimes he made them pay more than they should. So Matthew did not have many friends. But Jesus wanted to be Matthew's friend. He wanted Matthew to help Him. "Come. Follow Me." Jesus is telling Matthew. The people are surprised. They are even more surprised when Matthew gets up and follows Jesus. Matthew is glad to have a friend like Jesus. He is glad to be Jesus' helper. That is much better than making people pay taxes!

A TIME TO SHARE
1. *What work did Matthew do?*
2. *Did Matthew have many friends? Why not?*
3. *Who was Matthew's friend?*
4. *Aren't you glad Jesus is your friend too?*

WHAT DO YOU SEE?

Can you find a ship? Can you find a cart? What else do
you see that you do not have?

WHAT DO YOU SEE?

Do these men look like they are having a good time? Do they look like they are being kind to Jesus?

Jesus Eats with Matthew

Luke 5:29-32

Do you remember Matthew? He was the man who made people pay taxes. Jesus asked him to be His helper. Now Jesus is at Matthew's house. Some other people are there too. They are Matthew's friends. They make people pay taxes as Matthew did. But look! Some Pharisees have stopped at Matthew's house. The Pharisees are leaders who say they know much about God. They hate Matthew and his friends. They hate anyone who does Matthew's kind of work. "Why do you eat with such bad people?" these men asked Jesus. "Bad people need God too!" said Jesus. Jesus wants everyone to love God. He wants you and me to love Him too.

A TIME TO SHARE

1. What did these men say to Jesus?

2. What did Jesus tell them?

3. Jesus wants you to love God. Do you?

Jesus Helps a Man Walk

John 5:1-13

"Do you want to be well?" Jesus is asking this man. The man has not walked for many years. What do you think he is saying to Jesus? "Yes! But no one can help me," he tells Jesus. "Pick up your mat-bed and walk home!" Jesus tells the man. Suddenly the man knows he is well. He can walk. He is so happy that he goes to God's house. There he thanks God for making him well.

A TIME TO SHARE
1. *What was wrong with this man?*
2. *What did Jesus do?*
3. *Where did the man go when Jesus healed him?*
4. *Do you thank God when He helps you?*

WHAT DO YOU SEE?

Do you see the pool of water? It was not a swimming pool. People carried water from pools to their houses. They did not have pipes with water in them as you do.

Jesus Heals a Man's Hand

Matthew 12:9-14

Do you see the man holding out his hand? His hand was crippled. He could not use it. How would you like to have a hand you could not use? Wouldn't you want it to be healed? The man wanted Jesus to heal his hand. So Jesus healed it. Don't you think everyone should be happy now? They should. But some men are not happy. Do you see them? They are angry. They and their friends have a rule. This rule says healing is wrong to do on this special day. Jesus said their rule was wrong. It was more important to help this poor man than to keep their rule. That's why Jesus healed this man. Aren't you glad Jesus loves people that much?

A TIME TO SHARE
1. What did Jesus do here?
2. Do you think Jesus loves this man?
3. Do you think Jesus loves you?
4. Are you glad Jesus loves you?

WHAT DO YOU SEE?

How many men do you see? How many do you think are
happy? How many are not happy?

Jesus Teaches from a Boat

Mark 3:7-12; 4:1

Do you know what Jesus is doing in that boat? He is teaching. Wouldn't you like to sit with those people and listen to Him? What do you think you would hear? Sometimes Jesus tells a story. His stories are teaching stories. They tell about God. They tell about Jesus' home in heaven. They tell us how we can please God. You can listen to one of Jesus' stories. Someone can read it to you!

A TIME TO SHARE

1. *What is Jesus doing?*
2. *What did Jesus tell in His stories?*
3. *Do you like to listen to Jesus' stories?*

WHAT DO YOU SEE?
Do you see the water? This is a big lake. It is called the
Sea of Galilee. Jesus did many things here.

WHAT DO YOU SEE?

Look at the faces of these 12 men. What kind of people do you think they were? One man turned against Jesus. His name was Judas. Can you find him?

238

Men Who Helped Jesus

Mark 3:13-19

Can you count these men? How many do you
find? Point to Peter, Andrew, James, and John.
They fished for a living. Then Jesus asked them
to help do His work. Do you see Matthew? He
made people pay taxes. Jesus asked Matthew
to help do His work too. When Jesus told Philip
to work with Him, Philip was excited. He told
his friend Nathanael about Jesus. Then the two
men went with Jesus. The other men gave up
their work too. They went with Jesus. They listened to Him teach. They helped Him do His
work. Later these 12 men were called "The
Twelve Apostles."

A TIME TO SHARE
1. *What did these men do for Jesus?*
2. *What did they give up to help Jesus?*
3. *Do you like to do things to help Jesus?*

WHAT DO YOU SEE?

Can you find a chariot? Can you find a horse? Do you think they belong to Jesus? Do you think they belong to Jesus' friend? Do you think they belong to the soldier? Why do you think that?

240

Jesus Helps a Soldier

Luke 7:1-10

That man with the big hat is a soldier. He is an important man. He tells many other soldiers what to do. "Go here!" he says. The soldiers go. "Do this!" he says. The soldiers do it. They do not even ask why. But sometimes important soldiers have trouble. This man's helper is sick. Jesus listens to the soldier. "You do not need to come to my house," the soldier tells Jesus. "Just say that my helper is well. Then he will be well." When Jesus saw that the man believed in Him, He healed the helper.

A TIME TO SHARE

1. How do you know this man is a soldier?

2. What did he want Jesus to do?

3. Did he believe Jesus could do it?

4. What do you believe Jesus can do for you?

WHAT DO YOU SEE?

What do you see that tells that the wind is blowing? Look at the waves. Look at the men's clothing. Look at the sail of the ship.

242

Jesus Makes a Storm Stop

Mark 4:35-41

The men in that boat are afraid! Look at the waves. Look how the boat is almost sinking. Wouldn't you be afraid if you were in that boat? But Jesus isn't afraid. Do you see Him standing there? He is telling the storm to be quiet. "Shhh! Be still!" Jesus is saying. As soon as He says that, the storm will stop. The big waves will be quiet. Can you do that? Can any of your friends do that? Can anyone but Jesus do that?

A TIME TO SHARE
1. *What is Jesus saying to the storm?*
2. *Will the storm obey Him?*
3. *Will you do what Jesus says?*

This Girl Is Alive Now!

Mark 5:21-24, 35-43

Now here is a happy family! They should be happy. Something wonderful has just happened. Only a little while before, this little girl was dead. Her mother and father were so sad. Wouldn't you be sad if someone in your family died? Of course you would. But what could the mother and father do? Who could help them? But look! Jesus is here! He is talking to the little girl. "You may get up now," Jesus says. The little girl is sitting up. She is alive again. Don't you think this family should be happy?

A TIME TO SHARE
1. *What was wrong with this girl?*
2. *What did Jesus do?*
3. *Can Jesus do anything?*
4. *Do you thank Jesus for things He does?*

WHAT DO YOU SEE?

This girl is 12 years old. Do you see her father? Do you see her mother? Point to them. Who else is there with them?

Jesus Feeds Hungry People

Mark 6:30-44

Would your mother invite 5,000 people to dinner? Can't you hear her ask, "What will we feed them?" That's what Jesus' disciples asked when Jesus invited 5,000 people for dinner. But look who brought his lunch! Do you see the boy giving it to Jesus? It isn't much, only five little loaves of bread and two fish. But it is all the food that anyone has here. What will Jesus feed all these hungry people? Look at them waiting for something. Jesus thanks God for this food and begins to break it into pieces. He keeps on breaking pieces from the bread and fish. Before long He has broken enough to feed all those 5,000 people. Jesus feeds hungry people. He even helps to feed you and me.

A TIME TO SHARE
1. *What did Jesus feed to the 5,000 people?*
2. *Who helps you get your food each day?*
3. *Do you thank Him? Would you like to now?*

WHAT DO YOU SEE?

Do you see all the people? Do you see the boy's lunch?
What else do you see in this picture?

Jesus Walks on Water

Matthew 14:22-33

Is Jesus walking on a beach? No, He isn't. He is in the middle of a big lake. He is walking on top of the water. Peter sees Jesus. He wants to do this too. But look what is happening to him! "Help me!" Peter calls to Jesus. Peter is sinking in the water. But Jesus takes Peter's hand. He will not let Peter sink. Jesus' friends watch this from their boat. Do you see them? "You are God's Son!" they tell Jesus. Only God's Son could do this. Aren't you glad God's Son is your best Friend?

A TIME TO SHARE
1. *Why could Jesus walk on the water?*
2. *Why did Peter start to sink?*
3. *Who did Jesus' friends say He is?*
4. *Have you asked Jesus to be your best Friend?*

WHAT DO YOU SEE?
Do you see the men on the boat? How many can you count? What do they tell Jesus?

Jesus Heals Many People

Mark 6:53-56

Look at all those people. Everywhere Jesus went people crowded around Him. Many were sick. They knew Jesus could heal them. Nobody else could do that. That's because nobody else is God's Son. Only God's Son can heal sick people or bring dead people back to life. You believe Jesus is God's Son, don't you? You believe He is the Saviour, don't you? But many of these people did not believe that. Isn't that strange, when people saw Jesus heal sick people? What would you like to tell them?

A TIME TO SHARE

1. *Why did these people come to see Jesus?*
2. *How could Jesus heal them? Who is He?*
3. *Do you believe Jesus is the Saviour?*
4. *Do you believe Jesus is your Saviour?*

WHAT DO YOU SEE?

What kinds of people came to see Jesus? Can you find
some children? Where is a man with a pitchfork? Do you
see a shepherd? Where is a woman with a waterpot? Can
you find some men with fish?

Jesus Helps a Mother

Matthew 15:21-28

This poor woman needs help. Her daughter is sick. There are no good doctors. There are no hospitals. There are no good medicines. What can she do? "Help!" she says to Jesus. But the woman's daughter is back home. That is far away from here. Can Jesus heal someone so far away? "Your daughter is well!" Jesus tells the woman. The woman believes Jesus. She believes He did exactly what He said. When she gets home, she will find that is true. Her daughter will be well.

A TIME TO SHARE
1. *What does the woman want Jesus to do?*
2. *Does He do it?*
3. *Did the woman believe Jesus?*
4. *Do you believe Jesus will do what He says?*

WHAT DO YOU SEE?

How many people do you see in this picture? Do you
think this is in a town? What do you see that shows this
is in a town?

WHAT DO YOU SEE?
Do you see this man's friends and neighbors? Can you
find a house? What kind of country is this?

Jesus Heals a Deaf Man

Mark 7:32-37

"He can't hear! He can't talk!" That's what this man's friends told Jesus. Wouldn't that be sad? Think how you would feel if you could not hear or talk. The poor man could not even ask Jesus for help. His friends had to do that for him. "Please make our friend well," they asked Jesus. Do you see Jesus touching the man's ears? He also touched the man's tongue. Now the man can hear. He can talk. Don't you think he told many people about Jesus? Don't you think he thanked God often?

A TIME TO SHARE
1. *What was wrong with this man?*
2. *What did Jesus do to help him?*
3. *Do you think he told others about Jesus?*
4. *Do you tell others about Jesus?*
5. *Do you thank God often that you can talk?*

Jesus Talks with Peter

Matthew 16:13-16

Do you remember Jesus' 12 special friends? They are called "The Twelve Apostles." Here they are with Jesus. Can you count them? Jesus is talking with Peter. He is one of the 12 men. "Do you know who I am?" Jesus asked. Peter knew that He was Jesus. But Peter knew something more. "You are God's Son!" Peter said. Many people, who lived then, did not know that Jesus is God's Son. Many people now do not know it either. That's why we should tell them.

A TIME TO SHARE
1. *What did Peter tell Jesus?*
2. *Do you think Jesus is God's Son?*
3. *Do you tell others about Jesus?*

WHAT DO YOU SEE?

Do you see the mountain behind the men? This is a very tall mountain. It is called Mount Hermon. Often it has snow on its top. Today people ski on this mountain.

WHAT DO YOU SEE?

Jesus is showing Peter, James, and John that He is more than a man. He is God's Son. That's why He is shining like a bright light. The light is brighter than a picture can show.

258

Jesus Looks Different

Matthew 17:1-9

What is happening? See the bright light? Jesus looks different too. This is a time when Jesus' face and clothing were bright and shining. It is called the Transfiguration. That's a big word, isn't it? Peter, James, and John look at Jesus. They see that His face is shining like the sun. They see that His clothes are white and bright. The other two men in white clothes are Moses and Elijah. Do you remember them? They have been in heaven many years. But they came back to earth to talk to Jesus. No wonder Peter, James, and John are down on their knees! If you saw what they see, you would get down on your knees too!

A TIME TO SHARE
1. *What is happening here?*
2. *Who are the other two men in white clothes?*
3. *What is Jesus showing His friends here?*
4. *What would you think if you saw this?*

WHAT DO YOU SEE?

Do you see the village? Can you find some mountains?
How many of Jesus' friends can you find?

260

Who Is Most Important?

Matthew 18:1-5

Who is first? Who is most important? Most people would say "I am!" Jesus' friends talked about being first. They argued a little about it. One man wanted to be the most important in heaven. But so did another! Jesus heard His friends talking. Now He is sitting down with them. He will talk about wanting to be first. He will ask a little child to sit down with Him. "You must be like God's little child," Jesus told them. God does not want people to act big or important. He wants us to please Him, as good children should please their parents.

A TIME TO SHARE
1. *What are these men talking about?*
2. *What did Jesus tell them?*
3. *Do you try to please your parents?*
4. *Do you try to please God?*

A Man Who Did Not Forgive

Matthew 18:21-35

Do you see that rich man standing there? He is a king. He is a very kind king too. A man borrowed 10 million dollars from him. But the man spent the money. He could not pay it back. "Forgive me!" the man begged. The king could have put the man in jail. But he didn't. He forgave him. "You do not have to pay me the money," the king told him. But that man saw a servant who owed him 2,000 dollars. "Forgive me!" the servant begged. This wicked man would not forgive him. He had the poor servant put into jail. Now the king is angry. He found out what happened. Do you see what is happening? The king told those soldiers to put that wicked man in jail.

A TIME TO SHARE
1. *Why is this king angry?*
2. *Do you want God to forgive you?*
3. *Do you forgive others?*

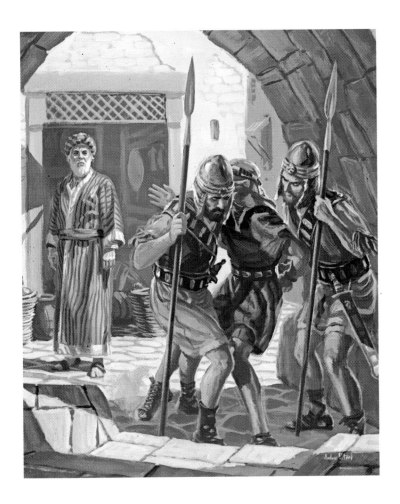

WHAT DO YOU SEE?

Do you see the man between the soldiers? He owed the king 10 million dollars. The king forgave him. But the man would not forgive a poor servant who owed him. Now you know why the king is angry. What else do you see in this picture?

Jesus Heals a Blind Man

John 9

This poor man is blind. He is poor because he can't work. He can't earn a living. In Jesus' time people did not hire blind men. So they had to beg for their money. It is sad to be blind. But look! Jesus is touching the man's eyes. He is putting some clay on them. Now the man will see. "You are God's Son!" the man will tell Jesus. Then he will bow down before Jesus. He will worship Jesus.

A TIME TO SHARE
1. *Why didn't this blind man work?*
2. *What is Jesus doing to him?*
3. *What will this man do now?*
4. *Do you thank Jesus for things He does?*

WHAT DO YOU SEE?

Point to some things the blind man will see. How many different things can you find?

A Good Neighbor

Luke 10:25-37

Do you have good neighbors? Usually we think that neighbors are the people next door or the people down the street. Jesus told a story about neighbors. In Jesus' story, a man went on a trip. But some robbers grabbed him and beat him. They took his money and left him. The poor man needed help but who would help him? One man came by. He was a teacher in God's house. But he did not stop to help. Another man came by. He was a helper in God's house. But he did not stop either. Then a Samaritan man came by. The hurt man and his friends had not tried to be friends with Samaritans. But this Samaritan stopped anyway. He took care of the man who was hurt. Do you think he was a good neighbor? Jesus did.

A TIME TO SHARE
1. *Who is the man carrying the hurt man?*
2. *Why was the Samaritan a good neighbor?*
3. *Are you a good neighbor?*
4. *Do you help others when they need you?*

WHAT DO YOU SEE?

Is this a crowded place or a lonely place? Why would robbers be in a place like this?

Mary and Martha

Luke 10:38-42

These two ladies are sisters. Martha is sweeping and cooking and cleaning and doing all kinds of things. Mary is sitting quietly, listening to Jesus. "Make her help me!" Martha complains to Jesus. But Jesus surprises Martha. "Listening to Me is more important than doing the chores," Jesus tells her. Martha can do the chores anytime. But she cannot listen to Jesus anytime. What do you think Martha will do now?

A TIME TO SHARE
1. *Which sister was busy with housework?*
2. *Which sister listened to Jesus?*
3. *Which did Jesus say was more important?*
4. *Do you take time each day to talk to Jesus?*

268

WHAT DO YOU SEE?

Do you see Martha's broom? How does it look different from your mother's broom? What else do you see in this house? How are these things different from things in your house?

WHAT DO YOU SEE?

How many disciples do you see? Do you see the water? It is a beautiful big lake. It is called the Sea of Galilee. Jesus did many wonderful things near this lake.

Jesus Teaches How to Pray

Luke 11:1-4

Shhh! Jesus is praying. He is talking to God. He is also telling His disciples how to pray. "Think about God, not yourselves," Jesus tells them. Then Jesus gave them a beautiful prayer. We often say it. It is called the Lord's Prayer. You may read it in your Bible.

A TIME TO SHARE

1. Ask someone to read Matthew 6:9-13.

2. Would you like to learn this prayer?

WHAT DO YOU SEE?

Do you see the shepherd? Point to him. Do you see the little lamb? Point to it. What two things does the shepherd have with him? Can you find them?

A Lost Sheep

Luke 15:3-6

Poor little lamb! It was safe at home with the shepherd awhile ago. But it wandered away from him. When the shepherd counted his sheep he found only 99. There should be 100. Then the shepherd knew that this little lamb was gone. He knew it had wandered away from him. Do you think this shepherd should leave his 99 sheep to look for 1 little lamb? He does. Now he has found his little lamb. He will carry it home in his arms. The little lamb will be safe with him. The shepherd is so happy. He tells his friends and neighbors, "I have found my little lamb. It is safe now!"

A TIME TO SHARE
1. *How did this little lamb get lost?*
2. *Who came to find it?*
3. *How are you like that little lamb?*
4. *How is Jesus like that shepherd?*

WHAT DO YOU SEE?

Look at the boy's clothes. What do you see? Why do you think he has patches on them? Do you see patches on the father's clothes? Why not?

A Boy Who Ran Away

Luke 15:11-24

This boy and his father are so happy to be together, aren't they? But it wasn't always that way. Not too long ago the boy wanted to run away. He wanted his father to give him lots of money. Then he could do things the way he wanted to do them. The father was a rich man. He gave the boy lots of money. Then the boy went far away. He spent all his money on foolish things. Suddenly he had no money left. "I'm hungry!" the boy said. But his father was not there to help him. The boy had to work hard. He often thought of his beautiful home. He often thought of his father. One day he came home. He asked his father to forgive him. Now do you see what is happening?

A TIME TO SHARE
1. *Where has this foolish boy been?*
2. *What did the boy ask his father to do here?*
3. *Do you ask God to forgive you?*

Lazarus Comes Back to Life

John 11:1-45

Do you know why Lazarus is wrapped up in cloth like that? He was dead! His sisters Mary and Martha buried him four days ago, on the day he died. They were so sad that Lazarus died! If only Jesus had come before. If only Jesus could have touched him and healed him. Then Jesus came. Mary and Martha thought it was too late to help Lazarus. But Jesus is God's Son! It is never too late for Him to help. "Lazarus, come out of there!" Jesus called. Lazarus walked out of the tomb. He was alive again. Now look how happy Mary and Martha are!

A TIME TO SHARE
1. *What did Jesus do here?*
2. *How could Jesus do that?*
3. *Do you believe that Jesus can do anything?*
4. *Aren't you glad Jesus has power over death?*

WHAT DO YOU SEE?

Do you see the big cave behind Lazarus? It is a tomb.
Lazarus was buried in there. Point to the cloth wound
around him. That's the way people were buried.

277

Jesus Helps Ten Lepers

Luke 17:11-19

Do you know what a leper is? A leper is a person who has a terrible disease called leprosy. Sore white spots come on the skin. In Jesus' time lepers had to stay way from everyone. They had to shout "Unclean! Unclean!" when people came near them. How would you feel if you had to do that? These 10 men had leprosy. "Help us!" they begged Jesus. Jesus did help them. Suddenly their leprosy was gone. What would you do then? Would you thank Jesus? That one man on his knees is thanking Jesus. But the others forgot.

A TIME TO SHARE

1. What was wrong with the 10 men?

2. What did Jesus do for them?

3. How many thanked Jesus?

4. Do you remember to thank Jesus?

WHAT DO YOU SEE?
Do you see the other men who had leprosy? What are they doing? What did they forget to do?

Two Men Pray at God's House

Luke 18:9-14

Two men are praying in God's house. The one in front thinks he is very good. He is telling God about the good things he does. He is not asking God to forgive him for things he did wrong. He thinks he is so good he does not need God to forgive him. But the man near the door knows he has done some bad things. He is asking God to forgive him. Which man do you think God will forgive?

A TIME TO SHARE
1. *Which man asked God to forgive him?*
2. *Do you think God forgave him?*
3. *Do you ask God to forgive you? Will He?*

WHAT DO YOU SEE?

What kind of building is this? It is God's house. What do
you think people should do here?

Jesus Loves Children

Mark 10:13-16

Wouldn't you like to be here? Everyone looks so happy. But wait! There are some men who don't look happy. "Jesus is too busy for children," they are saying. Jesus does not like that. "Let the children come to Me!" He is saying. "Don't send them away." Look at the children. They know Jesus loves them. You know that Jesus loves you too don't you?

A TIME TO SHARE
1. *What did these men say?*
2. *But what did Jesus say?*
3. *Do you think Jesus loves children?*
4. *Do you think Jesus loves you?*

WHAT DO YOU SEE?

Look at the cover of your book. This is the same picture with some changes. Do you see any toys or pets in this picture? Do you see some mothers? How many children can you count?

A Rich Young Man

Mark 10:17-31

Here is a man who is rich and important. You can see that he is rich because of his beautiful clothes. He came here to ask Jesus a question. "What must I do to live forever?" he asks. He is a good man. He tells Jesus he has obeyed all the rules in the Bible. But there is something more important than rules. If we want to live forever in heaven, we must love Jesus and follow Him. "Will you give up all your money and follow Me?" Jesus is asking. Do you know what that man will do? He will walk away. Jesus is sad. It is always sad when someone loves money more than Jesus. It is sad when someone loves any-thing more than Jesus.

A TIME TO SHARE
1. *What did this rich man want?*
2. *Why do you think he is a good man?*
3. *What did the rich man do?*
4. *Do you love Jesus and try to please Him?*

WHAT DO YOU SEE?

What do you see this man wearing? How is his clothing different from men's clothing now? Do you see the house? Point to it.

WHAT DO YOU SEE?

This is a picture of Jesus with two of His friends. What
kind of place do you think this is?

Jesus' Friends and Helpers

Matthew 20:20-28; Mark 10:35-45

Jesus had many friends. But He had 12 special friends. He asked them to go with Him. He asked them to be His helpers. They left their work. They followed Him. They went everywhere that Jesus went. One day two of these men, James and John, asked Jesus to make them important. They wanted to be more important than their friends. Do you know what Jesus said? "My friends who do My work should not want to be boss over others," Jesus said. "They should just want to do My work well." Jesus was saying that doing His work well makes people important to Him. When we are important to Jesus, that is best of all, isn't it?

A TIME TO SHARE

1. *What did James and John ask Jesus?*

2. *What did Jesus tell them?*

3. *Would you like to be Jesus' friend?*

4. *Would you like to be Jesus' helper?*

287

Jesus Helps a Man See

Mark 10:46-52

This blind man's name is Bartimaeus. Have you ever met anyone with that name? How would you like to be named Bartimaeus? Bartimaeus did not mind his name. But being blind made him sad. Blind people in Jesus' time could not earn money. They had to sit by a road and beg. Poor Bartimaeus! Who could help him? No doctor could open his blind eyes. But look! Someone is helping Bartimaeus. "Jesus, Jesus, help me!" Bartimaeus called to Jesus. "Help me see!" Jesus is telling Bartimaeus that he can see. How happy Bartimaeus is! He will jump up and praise God that he can see!

A TIME TO SHARE
1. *What did Bartimaeus want Jesus to do?*
2. *What did he do when Jesus helped him see?*
3. *Do you thank God each day that you can see?*

WHAT DO YOU SEE?

Look around you. What do you see? Which of these things could Bartimaeus see before Jesus helped him?

Jesus Forgives Zaccheus

Luke 19:1-10

Do you see that man up in a tree? His name is Zaccheus. But what is he doing there? Zaccheus wants to see Jesus. But he is short. He can't see over other people in the crowd. That's why he is up here in a tree. Now he can see Jesus go by. Jesus is talking to Zaccheus. He is telling Zaccheus to be His friend. Jesus will forgive the bad things Zaccheus has done.

A TIME TO SHARE
1. *Why is Zaccheus up in the tree?*
2. *What did Jesus tell him?*
3. *Will Jesus forgive you when you ask?*
4. *Have you asked Him to forgive you today?*

WHAT DO YOU SEE?
Point to Zaccheus up in the tree. How many other people
are there? Which one is Jesus?

Singing Praise to Jesus

Matthew 21:1-9

Jesus is riding that little donkey into Jerusalem. Look at all the people with Him! They are singing and shouting. They are waving palm branches. Some even put their cloaks on the path where He will ride. This is the way people welcome a new king. They think Jesus will be their new king. That's why they are singing and praising Him. When Jesus gets into Jerusalem some children will praise Him again. People are happy when they can praise Jesus. Aren't you?

A TIME TO SHARE
1. *What are these people doing?*
2. *Do you think they are happy?*
3. *Do you like to say good things about Jesus?*
4. *Do you like to sing about Jesus?*

WHAT DO YOU SEE?

What do you see the people doing to praise Jesus? Point to some people waving palm branches. Show some who are shouting or singing. Do you see some putting their cloaks on the path? How many have their hands raised to praise Him?

WHAT DO YOU SEE?

What do you see that is different from your church?
Point to these things.

Jesus Teaches in God's House

Matthew 21:10-27

Here is Jesus in God's house. It doesn't look like your church, does it? In Jesus' time God's house was called the temple. People came here to worship God. But there was no pulpit or communion table. There were no Sunday School classes. The temple had no Sunday School teachers. That's why you see Jesus teaching. He is telling the people about God. He is telling them about His home in heaven. Would you like to hear Jesus teach about these things?

A TIME TO SHARE
1. *What is Jesus doing here?*
2. *Where is He?*
3. *Do you like to go to God's house?*
4. *What do you learn there?*

WHAT DO YOU SEE?

Point to the poor woman's little coins. Do you think the man behind her is rich or poor? Why do you think that? Point to the money he will give. Can you find Jesus?

Giving at God's House

Mark 12:41-44

Do people pass an offering plate or basket in your church? Do you put money into it for God? These people are at God's house. Jesus is there. Do you see Him? He is watching people put money into that box with the horn-shaped openings. That box is like your church's offering plate. One man is rich. He puts in lots of money. But look at that poor woman. She is dropping two little coins into the box. "She gave the most!" Jesus said. Jesus' helpers are surprised. "The rich man has lots of money left," Jesus said. "But the poor woman gave all she has." Nobody can give more than that, can they?

A TIME TO SHARE
1. *What are these people doing?*
2. *Where are they?*
3. *Do you think this woman is happy to give?*
4. *Are you happy to give at God's house?*

WHAT DO YOU SEE?

Can you find the perfume jar? What do you see on the table? Look at the faces of the people there. What do you think each one is saying?

Mary Shows Love to Jesus

John 12:1-8

What do you do to show people that you love them? This woman is doing something you have probably never done. She is pouring perfume on Jesus' feet. She also poured some on His head. She is wiping His feet with her hair. Perhaps you remember her. She is Mary. Do you remember the time when her sister Martha worked while Mary listened to Jesus? Do you remember when Jesus brought Mary's brother Lazarus back to life? Jesus did many good things for Mary and her family. Now Mary wants to show Jesus that she loves Him. Jesus likes her beautiful gift. But your family and friends might like something different, don't you think?

A TIME TO SHARE
1. *What is Mary doing?*
2. *Why is she doing this?*
3. *How can you show people that you love them?*

Jesus Washes Peter's Feet

John 13:1-17, 34-35

What is Jesus doing? Aren't you surprised? Peter is surprised too. Jesus is washing Peter's feet. Peter does not like that. In Jesus' time slaves and servants did that. Someone as important as Jesus never washed someone's feet. But Jesus is doing it, isn't He? Do you know why? Jesus said the really truly important people are like servants. They try to help others. Jesus showed His disciples that even He liked to be a helper. Do you think we should do less than Jesus?

A TIME TO SHARE
1. *What is Jesus doing?*
2. *Who usually did this kind of work?*
3. *Why did Jesus do a helper's kind of work?*
4. *Do you like to be a good helper?*

300

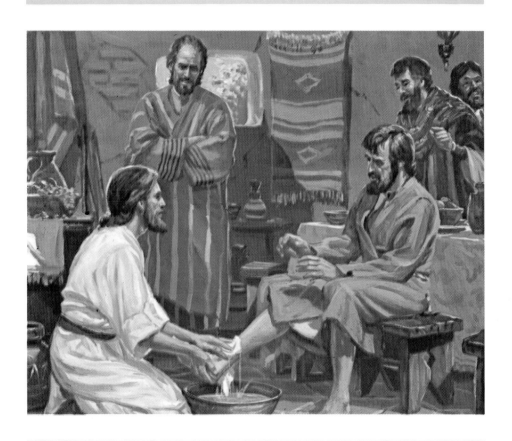

WHAT DO YOU SEE?

How do you know Jesus is washing Peter's feet? What do
you see? Point to the towel. Where is the basin of water?
What else do you see in this room?

Jesus' Last Supper

Luke 22:14-20

Each year Jesus' friends and neighbors had a special feast. It was called the Passover. People ate. They talked. They remembered to be glad for good things. Jesus and His friends are eating here. This is their Passover supper. But it is the last supper they will eat together before Jesus dies on the cross. "Drink this cup," Jesus tells them. "As you do, think how I will bleed for you when I die." Jesus gives them bread to eat. "Eat this bread," Jesus tells them. "As you do, think how My body will hurt for you when I die." Each time people in your church have Communion they remember what Jesus said at this Last Supper. They remember how Jesus died on the cross for them.

A TIME TO SHARE
1. What are these people doing here?
2. What did Jesus tell them to do?
3. Do you remember how Jesus died for you?

302

WHAT DO YOU SEE?

How do you know this is a supper? What do you see on the table? How many of Jesus' friends can you count here? Judas is not here. He has already left to make plans to hurt Jesus.

Jesus Prays in a Garden

Luke 22:39-46

Nobody is here but Jesus! His friends are not far away in this same garden. But they are asleep. Jesus is praying alone. He is talking with God about the next day. Jesus knows He will die on the cross. But He is glad that He can talk with God about these things now.

A TIME TO SHARE
1. *What is Jesus doing here?*
2. *Do you like to pray alone?*
3. *Do you sometimes like to pray with others?*

WHAT DO YOU SEE?

How many people do you see in this picture? Where are Jesus' friends?

WHAT DO YOU SEE?

Do you see the rooster? When this rooster crowed, it re-
minded Peter of something Jesus said. Jesus had told
Peter he would say bad things about Him. Jesus said
Peter would do this three times before a rooster crowed
that morning.

Peter Says Something Bad

Luke 22:54-62

This man by the fire is Peter. He is one of Jesus' best friends. But he is afraid now. Jesus has been captured. Do you see Him back there? Do you see the soldiers guarding Him? Some people want to hurt Jesus. Peter is afraid they might hurt him too. "I'm not Jesus' friend," Peter tells some people there. "I don't even know that Man." Then Peter sees Jesus. He sees Jesus looking at him. Jesus heard what Peter said. Do you know what Peter will do? He will run out of that place and cry. He will be sorry that he said Jesus is not his friend.

A TIME TO SHARE
1. *What did Peter say about Jesus?*
2. *Why did he say that?*
3. *Have you ever said something bad about Jesus?*
4. *Did you tell Him you were sorry?*

WHAT DO YOU SEE?

Point to Jesus. Do you see the thorns on His head? Do you see how His hands are tied? Point to some of the angry people. Can you find Pilate?

Jesus Goes before Pilate

Matthew 27:11-26

Do you see all those angry people? They want to hurt Jesus. Some want to kill Him. They have brought Jesus here to Pilate. He is the governor. He can tell soldiers to kill Jesus. Or he can tell them to let Jesus go. These angry people are shouting at Pilate. They are telling him to kill Jesus. Pilate does not want to kill Jesus. But he will tell the soldiers to do it. He is afraid of the crowd. He is afraid to do what he knows is right.

A TIME TO SHARE
1. *What do these angry people want?*
2. *Why will Pilate let Jesus be killed?*
3. *Do you ever do things you know are wrong?*
4. *Do you ask God to forgive you when you do?*

Jesus Dies on the Cross

Matthew 27:38-66

Look at Jesus on that cross! What is He doing there? This is the way people were punished for bad things they did. The other two men are being punished for bad things they did. But why is Jesus being punished? He never did any bad things. He is being punished for the bad things you and I have done. God would have to punish us for these things. But Jesus loves us so much that He came from heaven to be punished instead of us. God wanted Him to do this. Now we can ask God to forgive us for the bad things we did. He will because Jesus has already been punished instead of us. When we ask God to forgive us we can be Jesus' friends and helpers. Someday we can live with Jesus in His home in heaven. Would you like that?

A TIME TO SHARE
1. *Why were people put on crosses like this?*
2. *Why is Jesus on the cross?*
3. *Have you asked God to forgive you?*

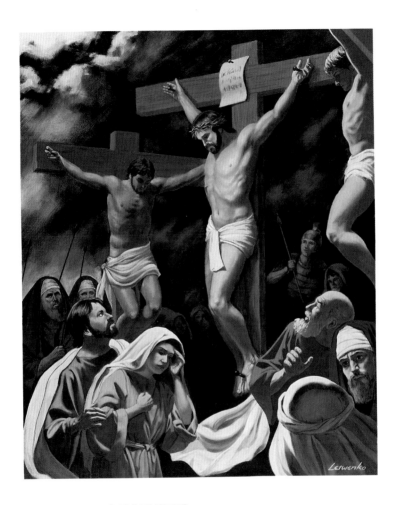

WHAT DO YOU SEE?

Point to Jesus. Point to the other two men. Do you see a
man helping a woman? That may be John helping Jesus'
mother, Mary.

Jesus Comes Back to Life

Matthew 28:1-10

These two ladies were with Jesus when He died. They were probably here at this tomb when Jesus' body was put inside. Now they are here to put spices on Jesus' body. But someone else is here! Do you see the angel? These ladies see the angel and they are afraid. "Don't be afraid!" the angel tells them. "Jesus is not here. He has come back to life!" What do you think these ladies will do now? They will run to tell this good news to their friends. Wouldn't you do that too?

A TIME TO SHARE
1. *What is the angel telling these ladies?*
2. *What will the ladies do now?*
3. *What should you do with news about Jesus?*

WHAT DO YOU SEE?

Do you see the big round stone? That was rolled across
the opening to the tomb. What do you see the ladies carrying?

313

WHAT DO YOU SEE?

Where are these men going? Point to the tomb. Is the
stone over the opening or rolled away from the opening?
Is Jesus inside that tomb? No! He is alive!

Jesus' Tomb Is Empty

John 20:1-10

Peter and John are excited. They are running as fast as they can go. But why are they running to that tomb? They have heard that Jesus has come back to life. Wouldn't you run fast to find out if this is true? You don't have to run fast to find out. These men saw Jesus alive! So did others. We know that Jesus came back to life. These men and their friends have told us that they saw Him. They are people we can believe. Aren't you glad Jesus came back to life? Now we know we will come back to life someday too.

A TIME TO SHARE
1. *Why are these men running to the tomb?*
2. *Will they find Jesus' body there?*
3. *Why not? What has happened?*
4. *Aren't you glad Jesus is alive?*

Mary Magdalene Sees Jesus

John 20:11-18

Do you see how happy Mary Magdalene is? Jesus was dead. She saw Him die on the cross. But now she sees Him alive. Mary is so happy that she doesn't know what to do. "Go tell My friends!" Jesus tells Mary. Mary knows now that she has some good news to tell. So she runs to tell her friends.

A TIME TO SHARE
1. *Who is talking to Jesus?*
2. *Why is she so excited?*
3. *What will she do now?*
4. *Do you tell your friends about Jesus?*

WHAT DO YOU SEE?

Look at Jesus' hands. What do you see? Those are scars. Men put nails through His hands when they put Him on the cross.

Jesus Walks with Two Friends

Luke 24:13-35

These two men walked from Jerusalem with
Jesus. But they did not know it was Jesus. Now
they do! Do you see how surprised they are?
They thought Jesus was dead. Now they are
seeing Him alive. They have walked with Him.
They have talked with Him. These men will
walk all the way back to Jerusalem. They can't
wait to tell their friends that Jesus is alive!

A TIME TO SHARE
1. *Why are these men surprised?*
2. *What will they do now?*
3. *Do you tell your friends that Jesus is alive?*

WHAT DO YOU SEE?

This is the room where these people eat. Think about the room where you eat your meals. How is this room different? What does this room have that your room has also?

Thomas Sees Jesus

John 20:24-29

Almost all of Jesus' friends believed that He is alive again. But Thomas did not believe it. "I must touch Him!" Thomas said. "I must touch the scars where the nails went through His hands. I must touch the scar where the sword went into His side." Thomas had not yet seen Jesus after He came back to life. But look! Jesus is now in the room with Thomas. Jesus came through the wall. He was suddenly there! "Touch Me!" Jesus says to Thomas. When Thomas sees Jesus, he knows it is true. Jesus is alive again!

A TIME TO SHARE
1. *Had Thomas seen Jesus alive before this?*
2. *What did Thomas want to do to believe?*
3. *Have you ever seen Jesus or touched Him?*
4. *Do you believe in Jesus?*

320

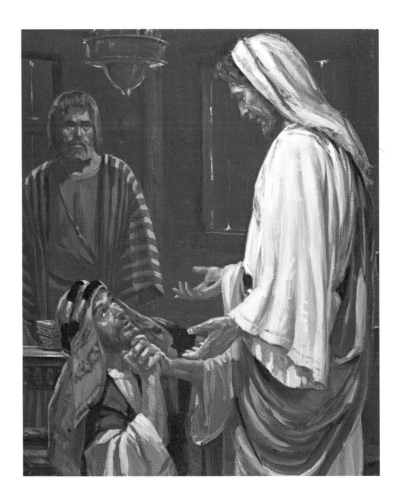

WHAT DO YOU SEE?

Look at Thomas' face. What do you think Thomas is saying? What is he thinking?

WHAT DO YOU SEE?

Point to the boat. That's where Peter was. He was helping his friends catch fish. They had not caught any till
Jesus came. He told them where to put the net. Then they
caught lots of fish. Do you see the net? It is filled with
fish.

Peter Sees Jesus

John 21:1-17

Peter is in a hurry to get to shore. He was in that boat. But he jumped into the water and swam to shore. Do you know why? Because Jesus is there. Do you see Him? This is only the third time Peter had seen Jesus since He came back to life. Peter can't wait till the boat comes to shore. He wants to see Jesus now. Jesus will tell Peter to help others learn about Jesus. Jesus wants Peter to be His helper. We also must help others know more about Him.

A TIME TO SHARE

1. *Why is Peter wading to shore?*
2. *What did Jesus tell Peter?*
3. *Do you want to help others know about Jesus?*

WHAT DO YOU SEE?

These people see Jesus going back into heaven. Do you
see the bright light? Do you see the clouds?

Jesus Goes Back to Heaven

Acts 1:9-11

Jesus is going up into the sky. He is going back to His home in heaven. He will live there with God. He will get a place ready for us. Someday He will come back. Then He will take those of us who love Him back to heaven with Him. He will take us to that special place He has ready for us. Do you love Jesus? Do you want to live with Him in His home in heaven someday?

A TIME TO SHARE
1. *Where is Jesus going?*
2. *What will He get ready there?*
3. *Will He come back to earth someday?*
4. *Who will He take with Him to heaven?*

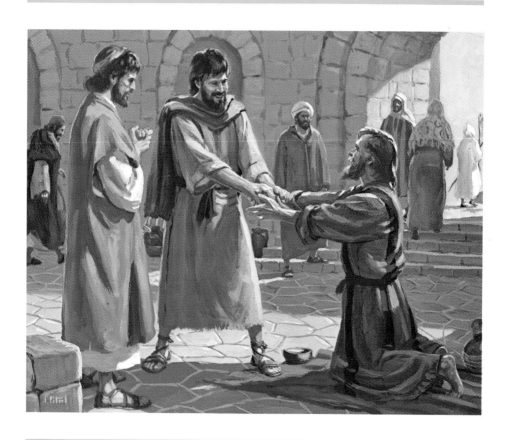

WHAT DO YOU SEE?

Do you see the big gateway? This was a big gate that
went into God's house. It was called the Beautiful Gate.
Look at the bowl which this man had. He wanted people
to drop money into this bowl.

God Heals a Crippled Man
Acts 3:1-11

That poor man on his knees has never walked. At that time people who couldn't walk couldn't work. No one wanted to hire them. All this man could do was beg. Here he sat by the gate that went into the temple, God's house. Each day he begged from people who came in. Peter and John have just come up here. They have no money to give the man. "But I have something better to give you," Peter is saying to the man. "In Jesus' name, get up and walk!" Do you see what is happening? Peter is touching the man's hand. He is getting up. Now the man will jump up and walk around God's house. He will thank God for healing him.

A TIME TO SHARE
1. *What is wrong with this man on his knees?*
2. *What will happen to him now?*
3. *When he is healed, what will the man do?*
4. *Do you thank God for special things?*

WHAT DO YOU SEE?

Can you point to Peter? He is the man holding the stick.
Do you see the man with the white beard? He was called
the high priest. He was the boss over many priests.

Peter Preaches about Jesus

Acts 5:12-42

"Don't preach about Jesus!" that man in the white beard told Peter and his friends. But Peter kept on telling people about Jesus. So the man with the white beard had Peter and his friends put into prison. He could do that because he was an important man. An angel let Peter and his friends out of prison. They went back to God's house. They preached about Jesus. Now this man with the white beard is very angry. "I told you not to preach about Jesus!" he is shouting. "We must do what God wants, not what you want!" Peter is telling the man. That's good for us to remember, isn't it?

A TIME TO SHARE
1. *What did the man tell Peter not to do?*
2. *What did Peter tell this man?*
3. *Should you do what God wants?*

Stephen Is a Brave Helper

Acts 6–7

Stephen was a good man. He helped people. He took food or money to people who needed it. He also told people about Jesus. Stephen was a good helper for Jesus. But some men did not like Stephen. That's because they did not want people to hear about Jesus. Some of these bad men wanted to hurt Stephen. But how could they do it? Then they had an idea. They would tell some men to lie about Stephen. These men told terrible lies. Do you see them there with Stephen? Now Stephen lifts his hands. He tells these people about Jesus. That makes these bad men angry. But Stephen is not afraid. He is a brave helper for Jesus. He will tell people about Jesus no matter what they do to him!

A TIME TO SHARE
1. *What kind of person was Stephen?*
2. *Why are these men lying about him?*
3. *Is Stephen afraid?*
4. *Are you afraid to tell others about Jesus?*

WHAT DO YOU SEE?

Do you see the man with the white hat? He is the high priest. He does not want people to preach about Jesus. If they do what Jesus says they will stop doing what he says.

Philip Teaches a Prince

Acts 8:26-40

Have you ever taught a prince about Jesus?
Not many of us have done that! But Philip did.
Philip was a teacher. He taught many people
about Jesus. One day an angel told Philip to go
to a road in the desert. Philip did not know
why he should do this. But he went. When an
angel tells us to do something, we should do it!
Suddenly a prince rides up in his chariot. Do
you see him? He is the man holding the scroll.
He can read this scroll, but he does not know
what it means. Then Philip tells him. The scroll
is telling about Jesus. Philip teaches the prince
about Jesus. He tells the prince how to be
Jesus' friend. Aren't you glad that Philip
taught this prince? Aren't you glad Philip
helped him become Jesus' friend?

A TIME TO SHARE
1. What did Philip help this prince do?
2. Have you helped someone become Jesus' friend?

WHAT DO YOU SEE?

Point to the chariot. How many horses are pulling it?
Which man is the prince? Which man is Philip? Do you
see the scroll? That is God's Word. Philip is teaching the
prince from this.

WHAT DO YOU SEE?
Do you see the bright light shining from heaven? It was so bright that it blinded Saul. What else do you see?

Saul Becomes Jesus' Friend

Acts 9:1-20

Saul did not like Jesus. He did not like Jesus' friends. He was angry when Jesus' friends told others about Jesus. He was so angry that he put some of them in jail. He hurt others. But Saul is not hurting anyone now. Do you see him kneeling there on the road? Saul can't see. A bright light is shining from heaven. Jesus is talking to Saul from His home in heaven. "Stop hurting Me!" Jesus is telling Saul. "Stop hurting My friends." Then Jesus tells Saul to go and help others become Jesus' friends. When Saul gets up he will not be angry at Jesus anymore. He will be Jesus' friend. He will help others become Jesus' friends.

A TIME TO SHARE
1. *Who talked to Saul from heaven?*
2. *What happened to Saul?*
3. *What will Saul do now?*
4. *Do you want others to become Jesus' friends?*

Dorcas Is a Good Helper

Acts 9:36-43

There is Dorcas. She is giving something again. Dorcas loved to be a helper. She sewed clothes for people who could not do it. She cooked food for people who were hungry. She cleaned houses or baked bread, or did whatever people needed. While she helped people she probably told them about Jesus. But one day Dorcas got sick. She got so sick that she died. Everyone was sad. "Find Peter!" someone said. Peter came. He saw how sad everyone was. He saw the good things Dorcas had done for people. Peter prayed to God. Then he said, "Dorcas, get up!" Dorcas got up. She was alive again. She was so happy to start helping again.

A TIME TO SHARE
1. *What did Dorcas do for people?*
2. *Do you think she liked to be a helper?*
3. *Do you like to be a helper?*

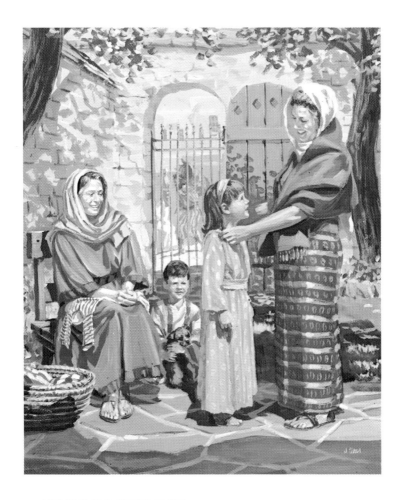

WHAT DO YOU SEE?

Do you see the mother and her two children? Do they look happy or sad? Point to Dorcas. Does she look happy or sad?

Cornelius Believes in Jesus
Acts 10

The soldier's name is Cornelius. He sent for
Peter. An angel told him to do this. Now Peter
is telling Cornelius about Jesus. Do you see
Cornelius' family and servants? They are listening to Peter too. Cornelius and his family
believed in Jesus as their Saviour.

A TIME TO SHARE
1. *What did Peter tell Cornelius?*
2. *What did Cornelius and his family do?*
3. *Do you believe in Jesus as your Saviour?*

WHAT DO YOU SEE?
Which lady do you think is Cornelius' wife? Which are
his children? The others are probably servants or other
relatives.

Peter Gets out of Prison

Acts 12:1-11

Look at those chains fall from Peter's wrists! He is surprised to see this too. But that person with him is an angel. The angel is taking Peter out of prison. God has more work for Peter to do. "Follow me!" the angel is telling Peter. Peter will follow the angel out into the street. He will not be in prison anymore. God can do anything, can't He?

A TIME TO SHARE
1. *What is this angel doing?*
2. *Why do you think Peter is surprised?*
3. *Is there anything God can't do?*

WHAT DO YOU SEE?

Can you find two sleeping guards? They do not see what
is happening here. Do you find the bars on the window?
Those kept people inside the prison.

Peter's Friends Pray for Him

Acts 12:12-17

Do you see Peter knocking on the gate? Peter's friends are here, inside the house. They are praying that God will take Peter out of prison. But Rhoda, the little girl, stops them. "Peter is out of prison. He is at the gate," Rhoda tells them. Peter's friends are surprised. They are praying for something. But they don't believe it has happened. Before long they will go find Peter. Then they will know that God answered their prayers.

A TIME TO SHARE

1. What did Peter's friends ask God to do?

2. Did they believe that God did it?

3. When you pray, do you believe God will hear?

WHAT DO YOU SEE?

Where is Peter? Where is Rhoda? What kind of house do you think this is? How can you tell?

Paul Helps a Crippled Man

Acts 14:8-18

That man jumping around never walked before this. Now he is excited. Paul told him to walk. Then God healed him. The man could walk. He could jump. He could run. Don't you see how surprised those other people are? They have never seen something like this happen before. They think Paul and his friend Barnabas are gods. "No!" Paul tells them. "We are just God's helpers." Paul was right. We must never tell people we are doing something that God is doing.

A TIME TO SHARE
1. *What happened to this crippled man?*
2. *What did the people think?*
3. *What did Paul tell them?*
4. *Do you ever say you did something God did?*

WHAT DO YOU SEE?
Where is this man's crutch? Is he using it now? Why not?

WHAT DO YOU SEE?

Do you see Lydia? Point to her. Do her clothes look nice?
Do you think she is poor or has plenty of money? Lydia
sells purple cloth. Rich people usually bought purple
cloth.

Lydia Is a Good Helper

Acts 16:11-15

Paul and his friend Silas are far from home. They are here in Philippi to tell people about Jesus. Lydia listens. She believes what they say about Jesus is true. Then Lydia asks Jesus to be her Saviour. Now she is asking Paul and Silas to stay at her home. They will have a good home to live in while they tell others about Jesus. Lydia is a good friend and helper.

A TIME TO SHARE

1. *What did Paul and Silas tell Lydia?*
2. *What did Lydia do when she heard?*
3. *How was Lydia a good friend and helper then?*
4. *Do you share your things for Jesus?*

A Jailer Believes in Jesus

Acts 16:16-34

Paul and his friend Silas were telling people about Jesus. But some men did not like that. They had Paul and Silas put into this jail. Most people would cry and complain if they were put into jail. But Paul and Silas sang and prayed. Suddenly God sent an earthquake. The doors of the jail opened. The chains that tied up Paul and Silas fell off. Do you see them there on the floor? Now the man in charge of the jail is afraid. He will be killed if these men run away. But Paul and Silas are not running away. They are staying here to tell this man about Jesus. "How can I be saved?" the jailer asks. "Believe on the Lord Jesus," Paul tells the jailer. The jailer will believe in Jesus. He will help his family believe too.

A TIME TO SHARE
1. *Why are Paul and Silas in this jail?*
2. *How did they get out of their chains?*
3. *What is the jailer asking them?*
4. *Do you believe in Jesus?*

WHAT DO YOU SEE?

Do you see the door of the jail? What has happened to it?
Point to the chains. They were used to tie up Paul and
Silas. Can you find the keys which the jailer used?

WHAT DO YOU SEE?
Do you see the buildings behind Paul? Athens had many
beautiful buildings. It was a beautiful city.

Paul Goes to Athens

Acts 17:16-34

This city is different from other cities where Paul has been. It is called Athens. The people here like to talk and talk and talk. They like to talk about new ways of thinking. But Paul has come here to tell people about Jesus. He wants people to believe in Jesus. He does not want to just talk and talk and talk. Paul tells these people that Jesus came back to life. Some people laugh at him. But some believe in Jesus. Paul is glad for those people who believe in Jesus. He is sad that some want to keep on talking.

A TIME TO SHARE
1. *Why did Paul come here to Athens?*
2. *What did the people of Athens want to do?*
3. *Did some believe in Jesus?*
4. *Are you happy when people believe in Jesus?*

Priscilla and Aquila

Acts 18:1-11

Do you see Paul sewing? He is making tents. That is the way Paul gets money. Paul's friends Priscilla and Aquila make tents too. They make tents all day. But Paul makes tents only part of the time. He goes out to preach about Jesus part of the time. Priscilla and Aquila do not go out to preach about Jesus. But they ask people to come to their home. They teach people there about Jesus. They ask preachers like Paul to stay at their home. That helps Paul spend more time preaching. Jesus' helpers can do different kinds of things for Him, can't they?

A TIME TO SHARE
1. *Why are these men sewing?*
2. *What does Paul do as Jesus' helper?*
3. *What do Priscilla and Aquila do as helpers?*
4. *What do you do as Jesus' helper?*

WHAT DO YOU SEE?

Point to the cloth these people use to make tents. Do you
see the needles? Where is the ball of heavy thread? What
else do you see in this house?

WHAT DO YOU SEE?

How many scrolls can you count? Scrolls cost lots of money. But these people love Jesus. They don't want to keep books that tell them to do bad things.

People Burn Some Books

Acts 19:17-20

Look at that big fire! Those are books that the people are burning. They are called scrolls. These books are long rolls. But why are they burning these books? These people did many bad things before. The books told them how to do these bad things. But now the people believe in Jesus. They do not want to do these bad things anymore. They want to do good things for Jesus.

A TIME TO SHARE
1. *What are these people doing?*
2. *Why are they burning their books?*
3. *Should Jesus' friends stop doing bad things?*
4. *Do you want to stop doing bad things?*

WHAT DO YOU SEE?

Do you see a place where Paul could get out of this jail?
Do you see the soldier? People like Paul had no way to
get out of jail.

God Keeps Paul Safe

Acts 23:12-24

Paul is in trouble. Some men were angry because he preached about Jesus. They had him put into jail. Soldiers keep him from getting out. But some of these angry men want to hurt him. Some say they will not eat or drink till they kill him. Paul's nephew heard what they said. Now he is telling Paul what these men said. When the captain in charge of the soldiers hears that, he will take Paul away. God will keep Paul safe for a long time. He wants Paul to tell others about Jesus.

A TIME TO SHARE
1. *Why is Paul in jail?*
2. *What do some angry men want to do to him?*
3. *How does God keep Paul safe?*
4. *Does God take care of you and keep you safe?*

God Takes Care of Paul

Acts 27

Paul is on a ship. He is on his way across an ocean. But do you see what is happening? Do you see the tall waves? Look at the people in the water. Paul's ship is in trouble. It is stuck on a sandbar in this terrible storm. Paul talks to God about this. God told Paul that he would not drown. The other men would not drown either. Paul thanks God for keeping him safe.

A TIME TO SHARE
1. *What is happening to the ocean here?*
2. *What did God tell Paul?*
3. *Will God keep Paul safe?*
4. *Do you thank God for taking care of you?*

WHAT DO YOU SEE?

Do you see the men in the water? How many can you point to? They are swimming to land. Others are floating on pieces of wood. God is keeping them safe.

Timothy Is a Good Helper

Acts 16:1-4; 17:10-15; 1 and 2 Timothy

That is Timothy's mother Eunice sitting with him. Grandmother Lois is standing by the table. They are helping Timothy read God's Word. It was on long rolls called scrolls. Timothy's mother and grandmother pray with him. They tell him about God. Later when Timothy was a young man Paul came to his town. He preached about Jesus. Timothy listened carefully. He asked Jesus to be his Saviour. Then Timothy went with Paul. Timothy became a good helper for Paul and Jesus. Timothy was glad now that his mother and grandmother taught him from God's Word when he was a boy. Are you glad when you can learn something from God's Word?

A TIME TO SHARE

1. What are Eunice and Lois doing?

2. What will Timothy do when Paul comes?

3. Do you think Timothy is glad for God's Word?

4. Are you glad that you can learn about Jesus?

WHAT DO YOU SEE?

What do you see on the table? Do you see the scroll?
Point to the yarn that Eunice is using. What else do you
see?

WHAT DO YOU SEE?

What kind of clothes is Philemon wearing?
What kind of house does he have? Do you think he is rich
or poor?

Onesimus Comes Back Home

Philemon

Do you see Philemon sitting there? He is a rich man. The young man is Philemon's slave. At that time people bought and sold slaves. It was like owning cattle. This young man Onesimus did not want to be a slave. He ran away from Philemon. He went to a big city. There he met Paul. Paul told Onesimus about Jesus. Onesimus asked Jesus to be his Saviour. Paul wrote a letter to his friend Philemon. He sent Onesimus back with the letter. "Please let Onesimus come back," Paul asked Philemon. "Please let him come back as a friend." Do you see Philemon reading Paul's letter? Do you see Onesimus waiting for Philemon to take him back? Philemon loves Jesus. He loves Paul. So he will love Onesimus too.

A TIME TO SHARE
1. *Who did Onesimus meet when he ran away?*
2. *What did Onesimus ask Jesus to do for him?*
3. *Do you think Philemon will love Onesimus?*
4. *Do you love others who love Jesus?*

What You Should Know About This Book

MY PICTURE READING BIBLE TO SEE AND SHARE is a unique book. Through this book you will acquaint your child with the Bible in ways that are fresh, but basic. This book will serve you best if you take time now to acquaint yourself with the following guidelines.

A Book with a Read-to-Me Approach

The "read-to-me" times we spend with our children are times of two-way warmth. No other experience in life will take its place, for it builds a wonderful bit of togetherness.

This book is written for your "read-to-me" times. It is different from an "I-can-read" book for early readers. You will find a focus on oral vocabulary rather than a beginning reader's vocabulary. The book is not vocabulary controlled, with words chosen from a controlled vocabulary list. Words used in this book are those you would ordinarily use in your daily conversations with preschool and early elementary children.

Using Tense to Involve the Child

You will find a deliberate shift in tense in this book. Most of the time, things that happened are presented in past tense. This is expected and it does not surprise you. We look back at a Bible event and relate what happened.

However you will often find an easy transition to present tense. This is a conscious effort to take the child back into the Bible story itself and relive it. Suddenly your child is taking part in the event as it happens. From the listening child's perspective, the event is not a past happening in a faraway place of another era and culture. It is something happening now with your child in a "you-are-there" experience. The child relates directly and immediately with the people, places, objects, and even the emotion and action of the moment. It is a vicarious experience. Educators tell us this kind of vicarious experience is the next best kind of learning to being there.

A shift of tense such as this makes past and present tenses servants. Tense accomplishes a learning purpose instead of demanding strict obedience to a rule.

Barriers to learning are removed, such as time, culture, and lifestyle differences. Your child is suddenly a vital part of a familiar Bible happening. It is easy to see how the Bible comes alive through this approach. To your child, Bible people become personal friends, not merely ancient names.

1. Response to Something a Bible Person Did

Do you remember the story of Simeon and Anna meeting Baby Jesus in the temple? Anna is excited to meet the Saviour. You will read that Anna will tell many about Jesus. A response builder is inserted, "We should each do that, shouldn't we?" It focuses on a physical response, to do what this Bible person did.

The action of the Bible person is exemplary. But the response helps that action "catch fire" in the child and motivates the child to follow that person's example.

2. Response to Something in the Picture

Another type of response builder appears in the story of the angels appearing to the shepherds the night Jesus was born. The reading begins, "These shepherds are looking at something strange." The reading could continue by telling what it is. Instead the question is asked, "Do you see it?" This asks the child to respond to this strange sight, the bright light in the picture.

Why not pause at this time and give the child the opportunity to find the bright light and point to it? Why not also linger awhile longer and talk about it with your child?

3. Response to the People in the Bible Story

The story "Going on Noah's Boat" tells about the time when Noah and the animals went on board the ark. Notice this response builder—"What would you have said to Noah when the rain began to fall?" This helps the child think about the Bible person. It stimulates the child to think of starting a conversation with that person, not merely hearing what that person did.

The response builder may reverse this process by asking the child what the Bible person would say to him or her. The response builder may also ask what the child would do if he or she were that Bible person.

4. Response that Gives a Setting for the Bible Story

"Have you been to a wedding?" The story "A Bride for Isaac" begins with this question. It helps the child think about weddings now and then. The story focuses on the contrast between marriage today and in Bible times. It helps the child understand the way Isaac got his bride and points to the difference in culture.

368

5. Response to the Teaching Purpose of the Story

Each story has a teaching purpose. It could be called a learning purpose. Often this emerges toward the end of the story, as a conclusion. Sometimes it unfolds step by step throughout the story. Occasionally the story begins with its purpose.

In the story "Gifts for God's House" for example, when people brought gifts to build the tabernacle, the teaching purpose is for us to want to give to God for His house. This story begins, "Do you like to give things to God? These people do." It clearly sets forth the teaching purpose of the story at the beginning.

The child is stimulated to think about that purpose as the story begins, and as it develops. Thus the purpose is kept before the child from beginning to end as you read the story.

You will find numerous response builders throughout these stories. Take time to pause and let the child respond. Don't be in a hurry to move on with the story too quickly, lest you lose the most important reason for reading the story—the child's response to it.

Action Stories—When Stories Are More Than Stories

There are 174 "stories" in this book. But they are more than stories in the traditional sense. You will discover some of the following differences.

A traditional story often follows one tense; past, present, or future. In these stories you will find a change in tense as described in the section "Using Tense to Involve the Child." You will recall how this section emphasizes the vicarious experience the child may have by entering into the event as it happens.

The use of response builders, as described in the section "Making Things Happen with Response Builders," is not typical in stories. These are also for the purpose of involving the child in the Bible event, then going a step further with a response to something specific.

These stories do not begin at one point of time and progress chronologically from beginning to end. Nor do they recall the full details of an event in an orderly fashion.

As the title of the book suggests, this is a picture Bible rather than a story Bible. Through pictures, and the child's interaction with these pictures, you and your child *discover* the story, rather than *read* it.

However, by the end of each story, your child will know what happened and who was involved. The child will know the story even though it has not been told in a traditional manner. In addition to the traditional story elements, the child will gain personal involvement and response. This extra dimension earns for the stories the title "Action Stories."

Picture Reading—More Basic than Reading Words

The Title of this book, MY PICTURE READING BIBLE TO SEE AND SHARE emphasizes picture reading. Usually the term "reading" suggests the recognition of words and their meanings. But there is a method of reading that is more basic than word reading. It is called picture reading.

We often neglect picture reading because it is not clearly defined in our educational systems. But it is so basic that even the very young child can do it and enjoy it. Through picture reading the young child's thoughts and imagination will be stimulated. Through picture reading the child is involved in the event and its people.

Sometimes you will find picture reading in the story itself. More often you will find it in the short section called "What Do You See" which follows each story. We hope to accomplish the following through picture reading.

1. Seeing Things That Are Often Passed By

Have you ever taken a walk with your child in the woods? Have you stopped to explore the texture of a leaf, the design in some bark, or the activities of a colony of ants? These things could easily be passed by, especially driving past these woods on an expressway.

But lingering here on a beautiful day with your child, you discover things seldom seen by most people. You and your child explore the fabric of God's creation and you are enriched by your discoveries.

One important function in picture reading is this lingering to look at things that are often passed by. You may stop to take an extra look at the way people dress, the expressions on their faces, or things they are doing. Or perhaps you may take time to look around a room to find objects that are different from these in your home.

Lingering to look at the unexpected is a way to build your child's imagination. Television focuses on fast activity, creating the misconception that faster is better. Where then will your child learn to linger with an adult and look for the little things that build imagination? You will find in this book the help you need for this important part of your child's life.

2. Comparing or Contrasting Things within the Picture

Your child learns from comparing or contrasting things, even within the same picture. For example, help the child compare or contrast the clothing of a Roman soldier with the clothing worn by others in the same picture. Or perhaps you may wish to contrast the colorful robe that Jacob gave to Joseph with the clothing worn by his brothers.

It is helpful also to compare or contrast facial expressions, one object with another, one action with another, or the place where someone is going with the place where that person has been.

3. Comparing or Contrasting Things with Life Today

The way we live and the way Bible people lived is quite different. Picture reading brings out the comparison and contrast between these two lifestyles.

A child will enjoy comparing or contrasting

objects in a Bible-time room with the objects in his or her own room. Your child may also enjoy comparing or contrasting transportation, homes, dress, or numerous other things.

Remember again to stop to talk with your child about these things. Life is different today, but is it necessarily better?

4. Enumerating Different Elements in the Picture

Children enjoy counting jars in a room or sheep in a field. This is more than a counting exercise. It is an opportunity to build an inquiring and observing mind. "Can you find six sheep?" stimulates the child to look for something he or she may ordinarily pass by in the picture. It is fun to make a game of finding certain things or counting them.

5. Involving the Child in the Visual Portrayal

A picture is the sum of many parts. It is the composite of many activities, or people, or objects. Help your child, through picture reading, to enter into the picture itself and see its various elements.

374

In the story of Ruth, your child will enjoy finding: (1) Ruth, (2) what Ruth is doing (gleaning), (3) the grain still standing, (4) the grain in bundles, and (5) Boaz and his friends watching Ruth at work.

Help your child through the picture reading experience to see these as parts of the whole picture, even though all parts may not be mentioned in the story. Too often we may be content to say, "This is a picture of Ruth picking up grain," and pass by without further comment. But this picture is much more and you will build imagination, an inquiring mind, and an observant child as you look for parts of the whole picture.

6. Finding Things Which Enrich the Story or Its Background

In the story "Samuel Anoints David" Samuel pours something on David's head. The picture shows this happening.

Through picture reading, including added information, your child learns that this is an animal horn, that it is decorative, that the substance poured is olive oil, that the pouring is called anointing, and that this is done to show that David will be the next king.

Each bit of information discovered helps the child understand the story background and thus the story itself. The picture becomes much more than "Samuel Anoints David." It is a composite of many things from the Bible background that come to focus on Samuel anointing David. Thus as the child learns the story he or she also learns background information that makes that story interesting and relevant.

7. Helping the Child Decide What He or She Would Do in This Situation

Sometimes the child is asked, "What would you do if you were here?" or, "What would you like to ask this person if you were here?" This kind of question is based on picture reading. Opinion or decision is based on the things the child sees.

Through this exercise you are teaching your child to observe before making a judgment or forming an opinion. That observation is not casual, but usually a time of finding several elements, discussing them with you, then forming an opinion about what he or she would like to ask or do if there.

8. Discovering Personal Application through Picture Reading

Most of the picture reading appears in the story itself or in the section "What Do You See?" which follows each story. Most of the application questions appear in the section "A Time to Share," which follows each story. Some application questions or comments appear in the story itself.

Picture reading lays a foundation. Application material such as "response builders" and application questions build on that foundation. This application material helps the child think about ways to change his or her life as a result of what has been seen and learned. The result may be changed attitudes or conduct.

A Time to Share

With each story is a short question-and-answer time called "A Time to Share." This is an opportunity for you to have a sharing time with your child. Questions are of several types. Some are purely factual, asking the child to recall something he or she has seen or learned Others seek reasons or purposes behind the facts learned. Still others seek to apply Bible truth to the child's life today.

Questions build a spirit of togetherness between you the asker and your child who answers. Building this important relationship is a sharing experience and thus the title "A Time to Share."

The title of this book, MY PICTURE READING BIBLE TO SEE AND SHARE highlights: (1) that this is a picture Bible more than a story Bible, (2) that picture reading is a vital part of the book, and

(3) that shared learning experiences between you the reader and your child the listener build relationships that are more important than mere facts.

The "Read-to-Me" approach builds this sharing experience, promoting a togetherness between the child and teacher or parent. Personal interaction is achieved in the context of learning and applying God's Word.

During this sharing time, do not hesitate to add your own questions or comments. You will find this book a vital, stimulating help for your Bible times with your child. But its best function may be to stimulate you to go beyond what it provides.

More than anything else, we hope this book will encourage your child to talk with you often about his or her relationship to Jesus Christ as Saviour and Lord. We hope also it will encourage you and your child to seek times of prayer together.